Everyone's Welcome

Everyone's Welcome

The Art of Living and Eating Allergen-Free

AMANDA ORLANDO

TOUCHWOOD

Edited by Meg Yamamoto
Designed and illustrated by Tree Abraham
All photos by Amanda Orlando except for photos on pages 8 and 19 by Karrie Kwong.

LIBRARY AND ARCHIVES CANADA CATALOGUING IN PUBLICATION

Orlando, Amanda, author

Everyone's welcome : the art of living and eating allergen-free / Amanda Orlando.

Issued in print and electronic formats.

ISBN 9781771512732 (hardcover)

1. Allergy—Diet therapy—Recipes. 2. Allergy. 3. Allergy—Prevention.
4. Cookbooks. I. Title. II. Title: Everyone's welcome.

RC588.D53O75 2019   641.5′6318   C20189063068   C20189063076

We gratefully acknowledge the financial support of the Government of Canada through the Canada Book Fund and the Province of British Columbia through the Book Publishing Tax Credit.

Canada

This book was produced using FSC®-certified, acid-free papers, processed chlorine-free and printed with soya-based inks.

Printed in China

23 22 21 20 19 1 2 3 4 5

For Lili and Jake

Contents

INTRODUCTION

MY MISSION IS TO INSPIRE CONFIDENCE in people living with food allergies. I do this by raising awareness, and by sharing safe recipes, kitchen hacks, travel tips, and my own life experiences (even the embarrassing or awkward ones); I also strive to unite people in the food-allergy community.

My blog, *Everyday Allergen-Free*, is a site for teens and adults living with food allergies. There are so many resources for parents of kids with food allergies, but I didn't feel there was much for me as a young adult. With my blog, I endeavour to have no filter and share it all, even the stuff no one wants to talk about, like dating, kissing, and the awkwardness of high school.

I was born with allergies to peanuts, nuts, dairy, legumes, soy, chicken, egg, and certain fruits. I grew out of the chicken, egg, and fruit allergies, but the rest remained. My brother is allergic to peanuts, nuts, and some shellfish, and my mom developed a peanut and nut allergy later in life. So, you could say we are a food allergy family.

Our home was never completely allergen-free, but we did work to prevent cross-contact in the kitchen and shared spaces, and we always considered each other when eating something one of the others was allergic to. We all ate vegan butter, but I drank rice milk while my brother drank dairy; my dad enjoyed roasted chestnuts but always ate them after we had gone to bed. My brother and I were taught from an early age that intentionality is important, and that you can eat freely so long as you consider the safety of the other person and don't put them at risk of coming into contact. We put different milks on our cereal and took different lunches to school but always ate the same meal at dinnertime.

I suffered six anaphylactic reactions requiring an EpiPen as a child, so I came to understand the need to protect myself and keep a watchful eye on my own actions and the actions of others around me. If someone in class was eating a PB&J sandwich and touched my desk, I would wipe it down. I might mention it to the person or choose to do it discreetly, but either way I would make sure it was done. My teachers also kept a watchful eye—my mom gave them all the Theresa Orlando training session before I started in their classes—and of course my friends and other allergic kids in the class were already educated.

Once I moved on to high school things changed. My cozy elementary school atmosphere was a dramatic contrast to the independence of this new phase of life. I still brought my lunch every day, but most kids bought pizza and fries from the cafeteria or went to the local pizza place. I often went too but always brought my own food. I suddenly felt like the strangeness of my allergies was amplified. People noticed the eczema on my hands, which I desperately tried to hide, and often pointed it out. There were so many teachers, and with four different classes per day, there was no way I could rely on them to help me manage. I had to navigate new social situations, and I had new friends to educate, which felt unusual since they hadn't all grown up with me.

Dating was a new cause of anxiety, though I was so quiet in Grades 9 and 10 that the issue didn't come up. Making close friends made me feel "normal" and supported, but when I came out of my shell and finally started dating, I had no idea how to communicate my allergies to the other person. It took a lot of trial and error to get the wording right and to hold myself with confidence while doing so. I'd habitually sweep the allergy issue under the rug, hoping no one would notice, while also hoping they'd take it seriously. As you can imagine, that didn't go smoothly.

Moving away to university was my plan from the age of 13. I stayed in an apartment-style residence at the University of Toronto and had three roommates. Again, this was a whole new learning experience for me—a new group of people, new classes, a new location, new types of parties, bars, and all kinds of things I couldn't have imagined. Staying in a dorm wasn't an option since the cafeteria would have posed too much of a challenge, and I needed to be able to eat more freely and without worry. But I didn't let that hold me back from having my university experience!

Now, as an adult, I'm constantly faced with new sets of challenges: starting a career and moving through different jobs at different companies, partaking in business travel, vendor dinners, etc. I've learned that our personal food allergy experience and education are never finished; each phase of life presents unique obstacles, challenges, and successes. It doesn't get easier as you get older—it just gets different. But as you mature and become more confident in your ability to care for yourself, you will experience personal growth too, so take comfort in that.

MY FOOD ALLERGY FAMILY

My family truly is obsessed with food. We've always made our own sauces, pickles, and preserves every summer. We enjoy slow food, things that have to simmer, fresh ingredients, herbs from the backyard, and talking about food constantly. My brother and I like to say that we aren't picky eaters; we care only whether the food is safe.

I think it's important to be open to trying new ingredients, cuisines, and dishes. If you're already limited by means beyond your control, why self-impose more limitations? This is of course totally up to the individual. You may be trying a new diet, or perhaps you're not eating meat for ethical reasons. There will always be some things you aren't comfortable experiencing, depending also on outside factors like the setting and environment. Tasting a new type of food in a crowded restaurant with loud music might not be your thing, and that's totally fine.

It's important for the family and friends of people with food allergies to support those individuals, and to make the home a safe place where they can eat without worry. This might mean not allowing certain foods in, making your own meals together as a family, or keeping shared spaces clean and tidy. The routine is up to each family or household individually, so do what works best for you.

AVOIDING CROSS-CONTAMINATION

Managing your food allergies means avoiding the allergen entirely, in all its forms. When cooking for yourself in your own home, you have control over

which foods enter your kitchen and how the food is prepared. But if you share your home with another person who does not have allergies and who may eat allergen-containing foods, there is risk of cross-contact. Similarly, if you are eating in someone else's home or at a restaurant, for example, there is also risk of cross-contact. Here's how cross-contamination, or cross-contact, occurs:

On surfaces: sharing a knife or cutting board, crumbs or spills on counters and stoves, unwashed spoon rests, or using the same spoon to cook different dishes.

While cleaning: Using an unclean sponge that was used to wash something with allergens, washing dishes in a sink full of water if the bottom of the sink has residue from unsafe food, or rinsing dishes instead of washing them with soap.

On hands: Eating or cooking something unsafe and then preparing the allergen-free meal without washing hands, using hand creams that contain unsafe ingredients, or sharing snack bowls.

In food: Products with a "may contain" warning, pantry staples (such as a bag of flour that was scooped with a dirty measuring cup, spices scooped with a dirty spoon, pinch bowls of salt), or condiments and jams that could have been scooped with a buttery or peanut buttery knife.

Diligence and mindfulness are the keys to creating a safe cooking environment. It does require some advance planning and thinking if you are not used to it, but everyone will be more comfortable, relaxed, and safer if you do the following:

Wash everything. The first thing to do is wash down all surfaces with either warm soapy water or kitchen cleaner. Wash (or rewash) the pots, pans, and utensils you plan to use. I generally throw them in the dishwasher just to be safe.

Wash your hands often.

Use a clean sponge and the dishwasher. Sponges can hold on to bacteria and allergens. If you used a sponge to wash something that had allergens on it, they could still be there when you wipe down something else. Use a new sponge to avoid smearing allergens around, and throw things in the dishwasher when possible. Avoid washing dishes in a tub of water because nothing will be rinsed off and residues may remain.

Read labels and share them with the allergic person. Even if it's a label for something that seems obvious, sending a picture of the label is worth it. It will make both of you feel more comfortable, and the allergic person will likely want to read any labels when they arrive regardless.

Consider whether foods have been contaminated and don't use them if you are unsure. Did you stick a used fork into the pickle jar? Did your peanut butter knife go into the jam jar?

Communicate with roommates and write the allergies out clearly. When I was in residence at university, one of my roommates also had allergies, so we wrote them out directly on the fridge with a whiteboard marker. There was a huge peanut with an X through it, and the message was very clear. But we also printed up a chart of the other allergens and their pseudonyms and taped it to the door. It takes people awhile to adjust and learn how to think like an allergic person, so help them along any way you can.

Always err on the side of caution. If you're uncertain about an ingredient, don't use it. It's better to be safe than sorry.

APPROACH OTHERS' DIETARY RESTRICTIONS WITH POSITIVITY

Consider your approach to accommodating food allergies or other dietary concerns such as veganism or eating gluten-free. Do you have a positive attitude toward it? The way we feel about cooking for or hosting people with dietary restrictions can often be conflicting. It's not unusual to hear people say that these diets are inconvenient or high maintenance, but if it's a friend or family member, don't you want to make that person feel welcome? Sometimes people may be excluded altogether if the host is not comfortable

accommodating them, but wouldn't it be better to just explain the situation and ask if those people want to bring their own food?

Inclusion can be a touchy subject for people who have lived with food allergies their whole life. Sitting at the peanut-free table alone as a kid or being uninvited to birthday parties leaves an imprint. As do patronizing remarks about feeling bad for those people or putting them on the spot about the specifics of what happens during a reaction, in front of a group of other people. Food should unite us, not make us feel alone. Sharing a meal is an intimate act, and with thoughtfulness and consideration, everyone should feel welcome.

ENTERTAINING

If you're hosting people with food allergies, refer to tips on avoiding cross-contamination (see page 10). Talk with the allergic people before planning the food. They may prefer to bring their own food, or you may be able to come up with a menu or dish that is safe for them. Let them know all the details of what you will be making so that both of you are well informed and prepared. Keep separate bowls of snacks or appetizers aside if you plan on having some unsafe items out as well. This will help avoid cross-contact when your other guests reach for the chip bowl. Don't be shy about asking for specifics and directions; there is a learning curve to thinking like people with food allergies. If they do choose to bring their own food, it's not an offence to you; it's a matter of personal comfort and trust.

If you are the person with food allergies, reach out to your hosts ahead of time so they have plenty of time to plan accordingly. Provide them an emailed list of your allergies, common names the allergens go by, and foods they are found in. Describe cross-contact and the severity of your allergies very clearly, and ask to read labels of products before use. Offer to contribute a dish to the meal or to help cook (depending on the occasion and your relationship). Don't be shy about describing your needs. If your host wants to have you over, they surely care about your safety and well-being.

PLAN YOUR FOOD

Pocket snacks

I always carry food in my purse, no matter where I'm going. Finding safe food is not a guarantee when you have allergies, so always be prepared. It could be something as basic as an apple or banana, a homemade muffin or baked good, or an individually packaged allergen-free snack.

Restaurants

Dining out can be a challenge when you have allergies because it's hard to know which restaurants to trust. Some take allergies seriously, have action plans in place, and communicate them well to the diner, though admittedly these are the minority. That's why people with allergies tend to become lifetime customers of restaurants they're comfortable eating at. It's not uncommon to encounter restaurants that openly say they don't want to or are unable to accommodate you, or that promise to but then botch the whole experience.

I'd much rather have a manager turn me away than feign understanding. Poor communication or lack of care can lead to an anaphylactic reaction, which is serious and can be prevented only by avoidance of allergens. It pays to take 15 minutes ahead of time to do your research. Large restaurant chains may be more likely to have allergy programs in place than stand-alone restaurants, but that is not always the case. It depends on whether the owners are dedicated to ensuring safe food, whether through their own self-education and internal communication or with the help of an outside company such as Dine Safe.

So, what steps should you take?

1. First, look for a restaurant that serves the type of food you know well and are comfortable with (for me it's usually salads, Italian, or sushi).
2. Call ahead, read reviews, and see if any allergy blogs have written about it. Then scan the menu. Does it look like most dishes contain nuts, cheese, or whichever allergen you need to avoid? If the answer is yes, try somewhere else. Some places have a note on their menu that the chef will not accommodate changes to the menu; those places are knocked off the list right away. If they mention guests with food allergies in a positive way, they're pushed up to the top.
3. Next, make a reservation and note your allergies so that the chef can know ahead of time. Try not to book at peak times, because it's easier for the chefs to work on a separate meal without cross-contact when the kitchen is not in busy mode.
4. Always bring your allergy cards. I started doing this about a year ago when I was travelling for work to non-English-speaking places, and the habit has stuck with me because I've noticed an improvement in how seriously my allergies are taken.
5. Speak with a manager if you feel the server does not understand. I like to inspect my food a little (or a lot) when it arrives to check for crumbs or things that may have snuck in. Don't be afraid to

send it back if you find something that shouldn't be there. Most importantly, if it arrives and you aren't comfortable, don't feel pressured to eat it. Dining out can be an anxiety-riddled experience, so take it at your own pace.

6. Sometimes things get awkward, so become a good actor and take it in stride. Going for lunch or dinner with colleagues has always been a stressful experience for me, not because of the company, but because they get to see me at my most vulnerable moment: when I'm ordering. When I know I have a function coming up, I spend so much energy worrying about whether they'll notice my long allergy order, if they'll ask a lot of questions, if those questions will be unintentionally rude, if I'll be branded high maintenance, if a reaction will happen in front of them, and on and on.

I remember a time I was really nervous when taking someone important out to dinner with two fellow colleagues. And of course I decided to invite our new VP and a director I didn't know well. Nothing calms allergy anxiety more than dining with strangers! I made a reservation at a restaurant I had been to three times before, let the staff know about my allergies, booked it for 6:30 p.m. (it usually filled up around 7:30), brought my allergy cards, and got there 15 minutes early. I spoke to the server, who spoke to the chef, who said everything would be fine, and I even placed my order ahead of time—the same two dishes I had eaten every time before. I had shit *under control*.

Half an hour into the meal, I was happily snacking away on my carpaccio while everyone shared olives and appetizers. And then I lifted a piece of arugula and found a smeared green pea. All I could think was, *What the actual fuck?* I discreetly (probably not discreetly at all) checked my hands for swelling and took a quick peek at my face in my phone screen, checking for hives. Everything seemed okay. I waved the server over and quickly showed her the pea. She took the plate away. No new plate arrived. Everyone continued to eat olives while I sat in silence, pretending to participate in the conversation.

Course two, the main. Plates of pasta arrived along with my kale salad, which had dried fruit and seeds all over it. I asked the server if the seeds had been in close contact with nuts. She checked and came back to take the plate away. By this point the table had noticed that I was sending multiple dishes back, looking extremely high maintenance. I felt my cheeks trying to turn red as my mind tried to keep them normal. A whole internal battle was taking place while outwardly I had a Stepford smile plastered on my face.

The whole table had finished their meals by the time my salad came, which was now piled sky high, as though to compensate for the mistake. It was easily enough salad for three people. I could see everyone fidgeting because it was time to go, and I was just delivered the great pyramid of kale and cabbage. So I asked for it to be wrapped up to go. By the time I got home I was mortified, certain I had turned off my new colleagues, and I was super annoyed at the restaurant. The only saving grace was that the place was so loud, crowded, and dimly lit that it was possible no one saw what was happening at all, distracted instead by the elbows prodding their sides and the house music assaulting their ears.

The main point of this story is that it was awkward, I got through it, and people don't think I'm any more of an oddball than they did before. These awkward situations are bound to happen as you grow up with allergies, but the most important thing to remember is to keep yourself safe. Take it in stride, be confident, and let it roll off.

Travel

Travel, much like restaurants, requires advance planning and research. Here are some tips to make allergy-friendly travelling easier:

Start out by travelling to countries where your native language is spoken and that aren't too far from home.

Branch out once you have experience. It's often more comfortable when you can easily communicate with hotel and restaurant staff about your allergies.

Have a picnic. When I'm travelling with my husband, friends, or family, I always like to plan a picnic day because it allows us to eat more freely and with less anxiety. I'll go to the grocery store and grab my favourite fruits, veggies, and snacks, and whoever I'm with will do the same or pick up takeout. Spend some time grazing and enjoying the outdoors. It's much less stressful than a busy restaurant at lunch hour and is often my most enjoyed part of the trip.

Rent a place with a kitchen. If going away for more than a few days, this is advised. You never know when securing safe food will be an issue, and there's nothing worse than feeling starved while you're supposed to be on vacation or on a business trip. Airbnb, a rental apartment, or a hotel room with a small kitchen are all good options.

Bring staples from home. As you may already know if you watch the *Everyday Allergen-Free* Instagram stories, I travel with quite a bit of food. I need to know that there are always some safe foods for me to fall back on, both on the plane and when I arrive at my destination. I bring instant coffee, mint tea, tins of tuna, a small bag of oatmeal, Enjoy Life chewy bars, and some homemade items like banana bread or scones. And sometimes I bring even more than that, depending on where I'm headed and the nature of the trip. I also always request an electric kettle in my room, just in case I can't find a safe meal; there's always oatmeal with Enjoy Life chocolate chips to fall back on. Bring whichever foods are most comfortable and convenient for you. When I arrive wherever I'm going, I go straight to a grocery store to stock up on fruits and veggies to keep in my room, along with paper plates and plastic utensils. I often pre-eat before going out to dinner, just in case. A worry-free meal is the best meal.

Plan restaurants ahead of time. As described in the previous section, restaurants should be planned out in advance as much as possible. Communicate over email with restaurants where possible, read reviews on other allergy blogs, and make reservations. I like to look for lists on other allergy blogs about where people ate successfully, and I make similar lists on *Everyday Allergen-Free* to share my experiences with readers. One of my best friends went so far as to map out our days on Google Maps with the restaurants plotted out on our routes so we'd arrive

in the right places at the right times. I wish I was that organized! Knowing where your meals will be is a big advantage over having to find a place when you're tired and hungry.

When flying, call ahead and check the allergy policy of the airline. Some airlines take a hard line with wanting to serve peanuts, and those should be avoided. Going into anaphylactic shock during a flight is a very dangerous situation. Always bring your own food that you know is safe; this is not the time to try something new. Bring wet wipes with you and give the seat, armrests, and other surfaces around you a wipe down to remove crumbs and residue.

Use translation cards. Bring a stack of disposable allergy cards translated into the languages spoken in the country you are visiting. There should be more than enough to get you through at least three meals a day for the duration of your trip.

Keep epinephrine and antihistamines close at hand. Do not store these in your checked luggage, as the temperature below the plane is not regulated and the epinephrine could be compromised. Keep them in your carry-on or purse. I always travel with four EpiPens and a box of Benadryl. I keep two EpiPens in my purse and two in my hotel room, so that if I lose my purse I still have a backup of all my medication. Don't assume that you can buy these products easily in other countries. We have access to them quite readily in North America, but EpiPens and Auvi-Qs are not available in many countries. Never leave home without them. If travelling somewhere very hot or cold, bring an insulated carrying case to regulate the temperature.

MANAGING ANXIETY AND SOCIAL SITUATIONS

For a long time, food allergies and mental health were not often discussed in the same sentence. Whenever I had a serious reaction over the years I'd be left with a lot of heavy feelings. I was developing obsessive habits and patterns, and I felt socially isolated and uneasy. As a teen I remember searching online for social studies done on people with food allergies; I wanted to know if others were feeling this way and if there was any research available on the topic. I wanted to be "a participant in a study" just so I could see the results. At the root of it I longed for validation from the medical community for what I was feeling.

Reaction PTSD. In January 2015 I suffered my most severe anaphylactic reaction and it changed my life forever. I'd had five reactions previously but none of them had affected me so deeply. It's one of the reasons I started blogging: I felt compelled to share my reaction story. That became the first blog post on my very old site that no longer exists (sorry not sorry). I had eaten a piece of bread, the same bread I had bought weekly for several years, and suddenly went into anaphylactic shock due to undeclared casein (dairy). Whether the ingredients were contaminated or the recipe changed and was not updated on the packaging, I'll never know.

Once the drugs at the hospital wore off, I felt a sense of dread, fragility, and vulnerability. That feeling stuck with me for a long time. I couldn't bring myself to enjoy food anymore. I felt claustrophobic, anxious, and nervous every time I took a bite of something. I started looking at every meal like it could be my last, amplifying the risk to exorbitant proportions. I saw anything packaged or from a restaurant as a death threat rather than just something to be careful around. And every time I was in traffic, on transit, or on a plane, I felt extremely claustrophobic and would feel faint. What if I had a reaction and couldn't get out?

There was a stark divide between my life before the reaction and my life after the reaction. Before the reaction I was able to enjoy restaurants regularly without being completely overwhelmed with fear. I didn't avoid social situations as often, I didn't skip travel, and I wasn't claustrophobic. If a server assured me that my meal was free from dairy, nuts, peanuts, and legumes, I trusted them and dug in. I used to be able to enjoy a few drinks without feeling panicked.

After the reaction, I felt uncomfortable in any place that I could get stuck: the subway, airplanes, on the highway in traffic, elevators. Alcohol became a trigger for nervousness and worry. I completely lost trust in anything packaged that wasn't made in a ded-

icated allergen-free facility. I ate boiled potatoes and spinach for breakfast, lunch, and dinner for about a month. I was too scared to eat anything else. I'd buy a loaf of bread and let it go bad on my counter without taking a single bite. I felt that if I was the one to suggest we eat in a restaurant, then bad luck was more likely to strike and I'd have another reaction. I was suddenly superstitious. My husband Brandon likes to say that I no longer ate with abandon, and he's right.

It's now been four years since that reaction and I have made significant improvements mentally. I now travel for work quite a bit, and I feel in control of the situation, not anxious. I dine out with my family more often, I buy the occasional packaged treat, and I don't panic and think I'm having a reaction every time I eat. There were a number of things I did to help myself get to this place, and they really made a difference. Below are suggestions for ways you too can find calm:

Exercise. I started taking spin class at least once per week and doing yoga more often. Prior to the reaction I had already been an active person, but I became much more dedicated after. Exercise is a great way to clear your mind, stay focused, and feel in control. For you it might be jogging, swimming, or Pilates. Whatever your flavour, exercise can help you regain the feeling of confidence.

Have a bath. Take time to relax alone. I like to have a bath every day or every other day. Whether I'm travelling or at home, it's my nightly ritual.

Read. Try reading in the bath (that's what I do). It's amazing how quickly time can pass when you're reading a good book. I find that getting really into a good book leaves me with more mental clarity. Specifically, I like reading either a book about the restaurant industry (try *Sous Chef* or anything by David Sedaris).

Try essential oils. There is so much you can do with essential oils. Burn them in an oil burner (you can get these at the Body Shop or home accessories stores) before taking a nap or take a bit of eucalyptus or lavender oil and rub it into your temples and all across your scalp. The scents will help relax you when you're coming down from an anxiety attack.

Do simple rituals, like making tea. Simple rituals help me feel calm. Heat the water, warm the cup, steep the tea, sip, relax. The warmth of the cup is comforting too. By the time this ritual is over, I can affirm to myself that I've been sitting here for 20 minutes and have not had a reaction.

Listen to podcasts. Have you ever tried a relaxation podcast or YouTube video? I also search for mindfulness meditations and deep sleep podcasts to listen to at any time. Just make sure you have headphones on to get the full effect.

Use affirmations. If you start having an anxiety attack, use logic to talk yourself down. Does my mouth feel itchy? Am I swelling up anywhere? Can I close my hands easily? Is my throat sore? Has anything happened to cause a reaction? Do I have hives? Did I read the label? Take a deep breath.

Schedule—and take—alone time. Even if I'm in the middle of a party, sometimes I just need a moment to be alone and repeat some affirmations. Step out of the room, go outside, or pop into the washroom. Give yourself space to be alone with your thoughts for a few minutes. I like to find a mirror to check my face quickly for hives or swelling. I'm always pleasantly surprised to see I'm not covered in hives. It's interesting how your mind can amplify your worries; sometimes you need to just see yourself so you can say, "Wow, I know I'm being ridiculous," then move on.

Consider therapy. Last year I told my allergist that I was interested in seeing a therapist to talk about my reaction anxiety. Honestly, I thought he was going to say I was overreacting. I hadn't known any of my other allergic friends to ever seek out help, or maybe they just didn't talk about it. He told me that kids as

young as three were going to therapy to learn how to manage their anxiety and that he could refer me to a few people who specialized in this type of treatment. I still haven't booked an appointment, but I know that if things get bad again I have somewhere to turn for professional help.

LIVING ALLERGEN-FREE IS A WORK-IN-PROGRESS

The real deal is that the most difficult part of dealing with my food allergies is managing my stress and anxiety. At times it does have a negative impact on my life, and at others it merely serves as an internal compass to guide me away from potential dangers. And a lot of the time I'm just so tired of all of it and I wish I could take a break from having allergies for even a day.

I'm tired of lying awake at night wondering if the hives I found on my back earlier are going to erupt into something more severe. If I drink from a glass, put it down and come back to it later, I'll immediately regret it because I don't know if it was really mine or if it was used by someone else, even if it's in my own home. As you can imagine this creates a lot of excess dishes to clean. Thank God for dishwashers.

And remember when the whole dishwasher issue was floating around the Internet a few months ago? I couldn't help but read the sensationalized articles about how allergens can live inside your dishwasher, even though I know my boyfriend rinses his things before he loads the washer. And even though we didn't have an allergen-free house for my entire childhood, I didn't have a single reaction from using our cutlery. But nevertheless I still started washing all the forks, knives, and spoons individually with soap after they were already clean. It took about three weeks of that before I came around to the idea that I didn't have to do that in my own home unless they weren't actually clean already.

Over the last few years my anxiety has gone in cycles, like highs and lows on a line chart. Sometimes it's really high and I can visualize it in my head; I know it's happening, but I feel like there's nothing I can do to shake it. The biggest concern for me is that sometimes I'm afraid to eat. I stack all my anxiety on this one central moment of taking "the bite" and am convinced that whatever it is I'm eating, even if I made it myself, has only a 50–50 chance of being safe. It's worse when I'm home alone, but, of course, I only improve when I force myself to be home alone to challenge it. To anyone without allergies the thought of eating a meal alone on your couch as "scary" is completely ridiculous. But for me, sometimes it can take a whole night to get through that meal, and then I feel a huge sense of pride when I see the empty plate.

Years ago, when I was in my late teens, not eating started becoming a habit. Coffee for breakfast with one cup of plain oatmeal, 12 glasses of water throughout the day, a half head of iceberg for lunch. Finally eat a proper meal when my parents get home from work. I lost a lot of weight and had to work really hard to break the habit I had established somewhat involuntarily. The challenge was that every time I tried to eat something outside my usual parameters I just couldn't bring myself to do it. Some people thought I had body image issues, but the real issue was that I was afraid to eat; I saw food as this massive negative thing in my life and I just wanted it to go away.

I'm getting really tired of the late-night Google searches to determine what certain additives are derived from and is this brand okay for me and do they have a real allergy statement. I feel a lot of anger when another person suffers a fatal reaction and I just think, *Holy shit, how do we not have a solution for this yet?* I get worried that a treatment will be developed, but that it'll only be available to people under a certain age and I'll be left in the dust. I get claustrophobic thinking that I'll have to deal with this for the rest of my life. But I also don't want to get my hopes up now that I know I'll never grow out of it. And, even more unsettling, I worry that doctors will determine it's contagious.

I haven't always been this way. For a long time I just lived somewhat normally. I wasn't afraid to eat, and my allergies didn't populate my thoughts all the time. I wasn't afraid to touch public surfaces; in fact, my friends used to think it was so gross that I'd eat a sandwich with my bare hands on the subway. I would love to be that gross sandwich-eating subway girl again. That girl was relaxed. That girl could have a few drinks and not have a panic attack or become fixated on worrying about something she ate six hours ago. I know I can get back to being in that state again because I've done it before.

On the *Everyday Allergen-Free* blog—and in publishing *Everyone's Welcome*—my main mission is to inspire confidence in people living with food allergies, and part of improving your confidence is to own your truths. My current truth is that at times I'm a nervous wreck, but I'm working on it.

Coming to Terms with Not Growing Out of It. One of my biggest personal challenges over the past year has been to come to terms with not growing out of my allergies. As a child I always held on to the hope that it could happen. That one day my test results would magically turn around and I'd be healed. But then I had a realization when I turned 26 that now I'm really an adult and this is not going to change. So I'd better make the most of it, look at it from a positive angle, and appreciate the things I can have.

It's very easy to get caught up in the anxiety that comes with having allergies, and to cling to the possibility that there is an end date to it. But in reality, this is likely how I will be for my whole life unless a cure is developed. As soon as it clicked for me, I felt claustrophobic and tired. Managing allergies can be a lot of work and takes careful and meticulous planning, especially when you divert from your routine. Everyone comes to terms with their own self and situation in their own time.

I wanted to mention this in this book because it's something that seems to get very little attention. Every year there's a new theory about food allergies, a new drug being tested, and so on. These are all positive developments, and of course I would be extremely happy if they found a cure, but it can feel gutting when nothing comes to fruition. I've found it helps to keep that information on the periphery of my mind, and to focus on being mindful and logical about the present. We have a lot to appreciate and be grateful for, right now.

Don't Let Your Allergies Hold You Back. Experience the life you want. Do everything you can imagine. And don't let your allergies hold you back from seeing the world and all it has to offer. It can be scary to move through different phases of life and all the challenges that accompany them. But you can do it. Be selective about your friends and keep the closest ones close. They will care for you and make you feel at home. Find a partner who cares about you and doesn't make you feel like your allergies are an inconvenience. It can be hard to find such a person, but when you do, it will be special. Don't be shy about communicating your allergies. People around you want to know so that they can avoid endangering you, and you don't do yourself any favours by not communicating fully. If you hold yourself with confidence, people will listen to and respect what you have to say. Food should unite and make everyone feel welcome.

Trusted Brands and Reaching Out to Food Companies

It's always a good idea to reach out to food companies if you are unsure whether or not a product contains allergens or may have been cross-contaminated with allergens. If their allergen statement is not visible on their website, send them an email clearly stating the product, product code (if applicable), and which allergens specifically you are inquiring about. Trusted brands for me include:

- **Dream (plant-based "milks" such as rice and coconut)**
- **Edward & Sons, Let's Do Organic**
- **Enjoy Life Foods**
- **Free2b**
- **FreeYumm**
- **Giddy Yoyo**
- **Holy Crap**
- **MadeGood**
- **Rodelle baking cocoa**
- **SuperSeedz**

ALLERGEN

In North America we recognize eight top allergens:

Peanuts

Peanuts are legumes, not nuts. Peanuts, peanut oil, peanut butter or dried peanut butter can often be found in energy bars, vegan foods, sauces, trail mixes, protein bars, chocolate bars, pastries and desserts, mole sauce, and more. A small percentage of people with peanut allergies are also allergic to other legumes (like me!).

Dairy

Examples include milk, cheese, butter, yogurt, cream, ghee (clarified butter), and additives such as lactose, casein, whey powder, lactic acid, and monostearate. In addition to dairy products such as ice cream, whipping cream, and kefir, dairy is commonly found in pastas, pastries, curries, packaged/processed or frozen foods, smoothies and shakes, chocolate and cocoa powder, breads, cakes, frosting, dressings and sauces, frozen turkey, curries, salads, and more. Some people with dairy allergies are also allergic to goat's milk (also like me!).

Nuts

Examples include cashews, pecans, Brazil nuts, almonds, pine nuts, and walnuts. They are often found in energy bars, vegan foods, sauces, trail mixes, protein bars, chocolate bars, coffees, pastries and desserts, mole sauce, and more. Some people with tree nut allergies are also allergic to coconut.

Eggs

In addition to whole eggs, yolks and whites, examples include albumin, meringue, and additives. Eggs are commonly found in egg noodles, pastas, pastries, baked goods and desserts, mayonnaise, Caesar dressing and other creamy dressings, old-fashioned ice cream, natural flavourings, and more.

OVERVIEW

Soy

Examples include tofu, miso, tamari, edamame, soy milk, soy sauce, soy lecithin, soybean oil, and soy flour. Soy is commonly found in vegan butters and spreads and as an additive in the vast majority of packaged/processed foods, sauces, soups, vegetable oil, vegan eggs, and more.

Wheat

Examples include flour (white, all-purpose, whole wheat, and cake and pastry flour), modified food starch, durum semolina, couscous, noodles, and bulgur. It is commonly found in pastas, tabbouleh, noodle dishes, soups, baked goods, desserts, matzo, crackers and cookies, as a thickener in soups and stews, and as an additive in many packaged and processed foods.

Fish

Examples include any swimming fish, such as tuna, salmon, Arctic char, bass, monkfish, or trout. Fish is commonly found in salads and pasta salads, tinned and packed in water or oil, fermented into fish sauce, in chowders and soups, grilled or fried, in fish sticks, as smoked salmon, and more.

Shellfish

Examples include any mollusc or crustacean, such as shrimp, mussels, clams, lobster, crab, oysters, or scallops. It is commonly found in crab cakes, pastas, stir-fries, sushi and sashimi, oyster sauce, dried shrimp, smoked oysters, and more.

The recipes in this book indicate which allergens they are free from using coloured icons; see the legend on page 27.

SUBSTITUTES
FOR THE TOP EIGHT ALLERGENS AND MORE

Butter alternatives

COCONUT OIL. Its sweet, tropical flavour lends itself well to chocolate desserts, coffees, savoury dishes with lime and cilantro, and baked goods like muffins and cookies. I like to cut it with a lighter fat such as canola oil because it can be a bit heavy or greasy. Some people with tree nut allergies are also allergic to coconut. This oil is suitable for vegetarians and vegans.

COCONUT BUTTER. It has a creamier, thicker texture than coconut oil and works well in energy balls, baking, and sauces, and spread on toast. Some people with tree nut allergies are also allergic to coconut. Coconut butter is suitable for vegetarians and vegans.

LARD. Made from beef fat, lard usually contains citric acid and BHT (a chemical that is often made from synthetic materials). It works really well in flaky pastries, crusts, and cookies, and has a very long shelf life. It doesn't have much of a taste but does provide a lot of texture. I often cut it with olive or coconut oil to add flavour. Lard is not suitable for vegetarians or vegans.

OLIVE OIL. Use in pastas, stir-fries, soups, stews, roasts, and even in baking. Olive oil can replace butter in nearly any savoury recipe. It has a low burn point, so avoid using it for deep-frying. Olives are not one of the top eight allergens, but be wary of cheap or impure olive oils that may be cut with vegetable oil, which often contains soy.

CANOLA OIL. Also called rapeseed oil, this is a grain-derived oil with a neutral flavour. It's perfect for cakes, muffins, baking, frying, deep-frying, dressings, and sauces. It is not a top eight allergen.

BUTTER SUBSTITUTES TO WATCH OUT FOR:
- **Vegan butters** are often made from soy or legumes such as pea and chickpea.
- **Vegetable shortening** is made from soybean oil.
- **Vegetable oil** is often a mix of canola, soybean, or sunflower seed oil.

CHEESE ALTERNATIVES. Daiya is a popular brand of vegan cheese made from legumes. It is suitable for vegetarians and vegans but not for people with a legume allergy.

CHEESE ALTERNATIVES TO WATCH OUT FOR:
- **Rice cheese** often has additives derived from dairy products.
- **Nut-based cheeses (cashew especially)** are growing in popularity. They tend to be vegetarian and vegan but do contain nuts.

Dairy milk alternatives

OAT MILK. The extremely mild flavour and thin texture of oat milk makes it best suited as a substitute for dairy milk in baking.

RICE MILK. My personal favourite milk alternative, rice milk is tasty on cereal, in tea or coffee, to bake with, to blend into a smoothie, or to drink on its own.

COCONUT MILK. The best in coffee! Coconut milk froths up really well and has a thick texture that mimics milk more closely than does any other substitute. Its creamy flavour is a great addition to hot drinks, cereal, soups and stir-fries, and in baking.

HEMP MILK. This milk alternative is a little earthy tasting with a distinct flavour. I reserve hemp milk mostly for baking and desserts.

SUN MILK. Very thick due to the oily texture of sunflower seeds, sun milk is a less common milk substitute. It can turn your baked goods and pancakes a slightly grey colour, so use it sparingly. My taste testers have either loved or hated sun milk.

WATCH OUT FOR: Almond, cashew, and soy milk are all popular vegan milk options but contain one or more of the top eight allergens. Pea protein can be added to vegan milks to add nutritional value, so be sure to keep that in mind if you have a legume allergy (like I do).

Sweeteners / sugar alternatives

MAPLE SYRUP. This is my favourite natural sweetener, although it can be pricy. It has a woody, warm flavour. Use in dressings and sauces or on pancakes, waffles, or meats. I would put maple syrup on nearly anything!

HONEY. Thicker, sweeter, and more floral, honey comes in so many varieties, and each one has a unique flavour. I like to add honey to cookie dough for a chewier texture, to salad dressings, and to my tea, or use it as a glaze on meats or to soothe a sore throat. I always buy organic honey because it truly does taste better.

MOLASSES. This sweetener is super thick and very rich in flavour. I reserve molasses for

baking and use it only when it's balanced by other spicy and complex flavours. Use it sparingly because it packs a punch of colour and flavour.

BROWN RICE SYRUP. This is a good, simple syrup to use in baking, but it does not offer the intensity of other sweeteners. It adds texture to oatmeal bars and other baked goods and has a mellow flavour.

AGAVE SYRUP. Derived from aloe, this sweetener can also run on the pricey side but makes a great addition to cocktails, dressings, and baked goods. It also works as a substitute for maple syrup on pancakes.

Egg alternatives

AT BREAKFAST: A good egg substitute doesn't have to be a protein source but can be of some other nutritional value. The main point is that it has body and substance. I often replace egg with sliced avocado or banana, or simply frame the meal so that it would not have been the star of the show. For example, serve a bowl of granola with fresh fruit and avocado, or candied bacon with a scone, fruit salad, and a smoothie.

EGG AND ALTERNATIVE PROTEIN SOURCES TO WATCH OUT FOR:
- **Tofu eggs**, which are often scrambled and are made of soy
- **Soy- and chickpea-based cheeses and egg substitutes**, which are made from legumes (lupin)
- **Cashew- or nut-based vegan cheeses**
- **Tahini and halvah**, which are derived from sesame seeds
- **Cashew- or almond-based vegan yogurts**
- **"High-protein" or gluten-free pastas**, which are often made from lentils, peas, or other legumes and may use egg as a binder.

EGG SUBSTITUTES FOR BAKING (ALL VEGETARIAN AND VEGAN):
- **Banana**. Use 1 banana plus ¼ tsp baking soda per egg. This works well in pancakes, quick breads, and muffins.
- **Sunflower seed butter**. Use 1 heaping tbsp per egg. This works best when replacing egg that was serving as a binder or emulsifier, for example, in cookies or dressings.
- **Aquafaba**. Believe it or not, this is actually bean water. Use 3 tbsp per egg. It can be whipped up like egg whites, so use it in recipes where frothy eggs are called for, such as soufflé pancakes, meringue, and macaroons.
- **Flax or chia seeds**. Mix 1 tbsp ground seeds with 3 tbsp water and let it sit until it becomes a little slimy looking. Use 1 tbsp flax or chia seeds per egg.
- **Unsweetened applesauce**. Use ⅓ cup applesauce plus ¼ tsp baking soda per egg. Use this in baking, especially cakes, muffins, quick breads, and pancakes.

Wheat alternatives

For bread or wraps, I generally use Boston or romaine lettuce. Firm polenta is also a good substitute.

COCONUT FLOUR. This flour has a rich and delicious flavour but tends to be heavy, a little grainy, and oily. If you bake solely with coconut flour, your desserts will be quite decadent, but the texture may suffer. This flour is best when mixed with something lighter, such as rice flour, to balance it out. People with tree nut allergies may be allergic to coconut.

RICE FLOUR. Very light and powdery, this flour makes my favourite type of gluten-free pasta and bakes well in cookies or other low-rise baked goods. Rice is not a top eight allergen.

SORGHUM FLOUR. Made from a ground-down grain, sorghum flour is generally mixed with other flours, such as rice and tapioca flour, to achieve a lighter consistency. Sorghum is not a top eight allergen.

OAT FLOUR. This can be gluten-free but depends on the brand and whether it was cross-contaminated with wheat flour. It cannot be used as a direct substitute for wheat flour but works well in a blend.

TAPIOCA FLOUR. This is usually added as a thickener to gluten-free flour blends and is made from a root vegetable. It contains none of the top eight allergens.

BUCKWHEAT FLOUR. This gluten-free flour has become increasingly popular in baking and contains none of the top eight allergens.

Unfortunately, no single alternative flour works as a direct substitute for wheat flour. The best way to bake gluten-free is to blend several flours and a thickener together, ideally rice flour with a heavier or fattier flour, such as coconut or buckwheat, and tapioca starch. A general rule in baking gluten-free is to mix one part tapioca starch with two parts other flours.

Baking gluten-free can be challenging as it's difficult to achieve the right texture and consistency with flours that resist rising. My tip is to focus on desserts or baked goods that don't call for much flour to begin with or that don't call for yeast. The results will be much more successful and flavourful. It's best to work with the natural inclinations of each ingredient to produce the best result.

The most popular allergens to watch for include almond, pea, and garbanzo or chickpea. Almond flour has become very popular over the last few years, as have gluten-free foods in general.

RECIPE LEGEND

All recipes indicate which allergens they are free from using the following coloured icons:

S Soy -free

P Peanut -free

W Wheat -free

N Nut -free

F Fish -free

D Dairy -free

SF Shellfish -free

E Egg -free

C Coconut -free

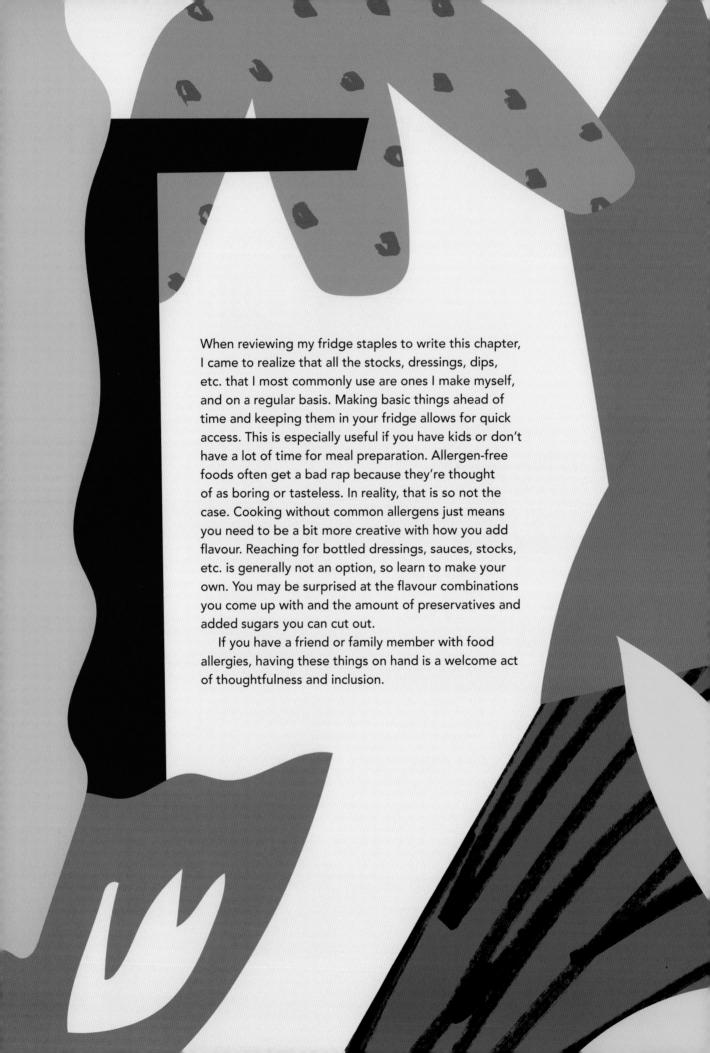

When reviewing my fridge staples to write this chapter, I came to realize that all the stocks, dressings, dips, etc. that I most commonly use are ones I make myself, and on a regular basis. Making basic things ahead of time and keeping them in your fridge allows for quick access. This is especially useful if you have kids or don't have a lot of time for meal preparation. Allergen-free foods often get a bad rap because they're thought of as boring or tasteless. In reality, that is so not the case. Cooking without common allergens just means you need to be a bit more creative with how you add flavour. Reaching for bottled dressings, sauces, stocks, etc. is generally not an option, so learn to make your own. You may be surprised at the flavour combinations you come up with and the amount of preservatives and added sugars you can cut out.

If you have a friend or family member with food allergies, having these things on hand is a welcome act of thoughtfulness and inclusion.

Basic Recipes

Chicken Broth

1 chicken carcass

1 cooking onion, peeled and left whole

3–4 sprigs fresh thyme

1 tsp salt

The next time you make a dinner of roast chicken (page 140), save the carcass for homemade stock. Put the carcass in a large pot and cover with water until it is fully submerged. Add the onion, thyme, and salt. Bring to a rolling boil, then reduce and simmer for a minimum of 4 hours. Strain and keep refrigerated up to 3 days in a Mason jar, or let cool and freeze. Ideal for soups, stews, polenta, and more.

MAKES 6-8 CUPS

Vegetable Broth

Vegetarian and vegan

3 stalks celery

2 large carrots

1 baking potato, peeled

1 onion, peeled

2 cloves garlic

3–4 sprigs fresh thyme

2–3 leaves sage

1 bay leaf

1 tsp sea salt

¼ tsp black pepper

Add all the ingredients to a large soup pot and fill with water so that everything is submerged. Bring to a boil, then put the lid on askew (so that steam can escape) and let simmer for 3–5 hours until it has reduced and becomes a nice deep earthy colour. You can either use it right away in your favourite soup recipe or keep it sealed in a jar in the fridge for up to 3 days.

MAKES 6-8 CUPS

Salad Dressings

One might not think of salad dressing as a place for potential allergens to hide, but they can be anywhere. I'm not one for bottled dressings even if they are safe for me, because I prefer the freshness of making my own. But I also know it's not unusual to find dressings that contain cheese, dairy-based additives, egg, and soy, and some less common allergens such as coconut, sesame, and mustard. Caesar dressing, for example, generally contains an egg base and sometimes Parmesan cheese. Ranch dressings are dairy-based, and many vegan dressings have a coconut or soy base. Just because a salad dressing looks creamy doesn't mean it must be made from dairy; it can also come from creamed/whipped egg, just as with mayonnaise.

Here are some examples of my favourite salad dressing combinations, using 1 part vinegar or acid to 2 parts oil (all seasonings to taste):

OLIVE OIL + BALSAMIC VINEGAR + SALT + PEPPER. A classic that never gets old. Add 1 part Dijon mustard for a creamier version if there is no mustard allergy. (Please note that Dijon mustard can sometimes contain gluten.) This dressing is nice on heartier lettuces such as romaine or on mixed field greens.

OLIVE OIL + LEMON JUICE + FRESH MINCED GARLIC + SALT + PEPPER. Blend or whisk all the ingredients together for a summery dressing that pairs well with lighter lettuces such as Boston or frisée.

AVOCADO OIL + RICE WINE VINEGAR + LIME JUICE + HIMALAYAN PINK SALT + FRESHLY GROUND BLACK PEPPER. Use this dressing for salads with avocado, berries, or other fresh fruit to balance out the sweetness.

OLIVE OIL + RED WINE VINEGAR + DIJON MUSTARD + SALT + PEPPER. This is your typical house dressing that pairs well with the mildest of lettuces: iceberg.

AVOCADO + OLIVE OR AVOCADO OIL + LIME OR LEMON JUICE + A DASH OF APPLE CIDER VINEGAR + FRESH GARLIC + SALT + PEPPER. Blend all the ingredients and use in place of Caesar dressing.

I tend to avoid using coconut oil in dressings unless it's a very refined product, as it can feel a bit too oily in combination with delicate vegetables. With any dressing, it's important to start out with less and add more if you feel it's needed. A soggy salad can't be turned around unless you have more greens to add to it.

Strawberry Jam

Vegetarian (vegan if maple syrup or sugar is used instead of honey)

4 cups strawberries

¼ cup organic honey or maple syrup

2 tbsp water

1 tbsp lemon or lime juice

½ tsp pure vanilla extract (optional)

Pinch of salt

Remove the tops of the strawberries and cut the berries into quarters. Add them to a medium-sized pot with the rest of the ingredients. Stir well, then cover and let simmer on low for about 15 minutes. Remove the lid and let simmer for 30–40 minutes, stirring often to prevent the jam from sticking and to break up the chunks of berries as they melt down. When done, the jam will be reduced, darker in colour, thick and sticky. Let it come to room temperature before scooping into jars. It keeps well in the fridge for a few days.

MAKES 1½-2 CUPS

Variations

You can replicate this recipe with blueberries, or use a mix of blueberries, blackberries, raspberries, and strawberries.

Honey or maple syrup can be replaced with the same measurement of regular white sugar, demerara, or brown sugar. Each one will result in a unique and different taste and a slightly different colour. My personal favourites are honey and maple syrup because of their complexity and the impact of the syrupy texture on the consistency of the jam. If you use powdered sugar (which usually contains cornstarch), the jam will be thicker and more opaque.

Applesauce

Vegetarian and vegan

3–4 large apples
(I prefer Crispin, Spy, McIntosh, or Spartan)

1 tbsp water

¼ tsp cinnamon

¼ tsp ground ginger

Pinch of ground clove

Peel, core, and roughly chop the apples. Add them to a medium-sized saucepan along with the water and spices. Simmer on low with the lid on for 30 minutes, stirring every 10 minutes. These varieties of apples will break apart on their own, forming a nice smooth sauce. Serve warm or keep covered in the fridge for up to 3 days.

MAKES 1-1½ CUPS

Tip
Applesauce can be used in baking, as a topping for pancakes (page 84), as a side dish with roasted meats, or on its own as a tasty breakfast or snack food.

Pumpkin Seed Butter

Vegetarian (vegan if maple syrup or sugar is used instead of honey)

1 cup unsalted, shelled pumpkin seeds (I use SuperSeedz brand)

2 tbsp pure maple syrup or honey

¼ tsp ground cinnamon or cayenne pepper (optional)

Generous pinch of salt

Up to ¼ cup oil (your choice of olive, canola, avocado, or sunflower)

Add all the ingredients, except the oil, to a blender or food processor and begin pulsing to break up the seeds into smaller chunks. Add the oil in a slow drizzle while the blender or food processor is working. You'll see the seeds become creamy and smooth. Add just enough oil to get it to a nice smooth consistency. You may not need the full ¼ cup.

Spread on toast or pancakes (page 84) or add to oatmeal (page 68) for extra protein and flavour. I also like to spread it on apple slices for a delicious afternoon snack.

MAKES 1¼ CUPS

Coconut Whipped Cream

Vegetarian (vegan if maple syrup or sugar is used instead of honey)

1 can (13 oz) pure, full-fat
coconut milk

2 tbsp powdered sugar

1 tbsp organic honey

½ tsp pure vanilla extract

Chill the whole can of coconut milk for a day before use so that the fat can firm up. Scoop out the fat and about 1 tbsp of the coconut water into a large metal mixing bowl. Ensure the bowl isn't warmer than room temperature, or the fat will melt. Add the sugar, honey, and vanilla and whip with an electric mixer until it's fluffy and creamy.

Spread on scones, use as frosting on cake, or add a dollop to your coffee for a bit of richness.

MAKES 1¾ CUPS

Other Fridge and Pantry Staples

- Allergen-free chocolate, such as Enjoy Life

- Butter substitutes: coconut cream, lard

- Citrus: lemons, limes, grapefruit, oranges

- Dijon and grainy mustards (Dijon mustard can sometimes contain gluten.)

- Dried fruits: figs, blueberries, cranberries, raisins

- Dried spices: cinnamon, cardamom, turmeric, ginger, fennel, black pepper, cayenne pepper, coriander, clove, bay leaf

- Flours: unbleached white flour, whole wheat flour, or a flour free of the top eight allergens, such as Gerb's Seeds Gluten-Free Flour; cornmeal

- Fresh herbs: basil, parsley, cilantro, dill, thyme, sage

- Fruit and veggies: sweet potatoes, yellow potatoes, carrots, celery, onions, garlic, peppers, berries, seasonal fruit

- Grains: basmati rice, brown rice, short-grain sticky rice, wild rice, quinoa, farro, pasta (pure durum wheat semolina)

- Milk substitutes: coconut milk, rice milk

- Oils: Extra-virgin olive oil, canola oil, sunflower oil, avocado oil, coconut oil

- Pumpkin seeds

- Pure cocoa powder

- Quick oats, steel-cut oats

- Sea salt, Himalayan pink salt, coarse salt

- Sunflower seed butter

- Sweeteners: dark brown sugar, powdered sugar, white sugar, organic honey, maple syrup

- Vinegars: balsamic, rice wine, red wine, apple cider

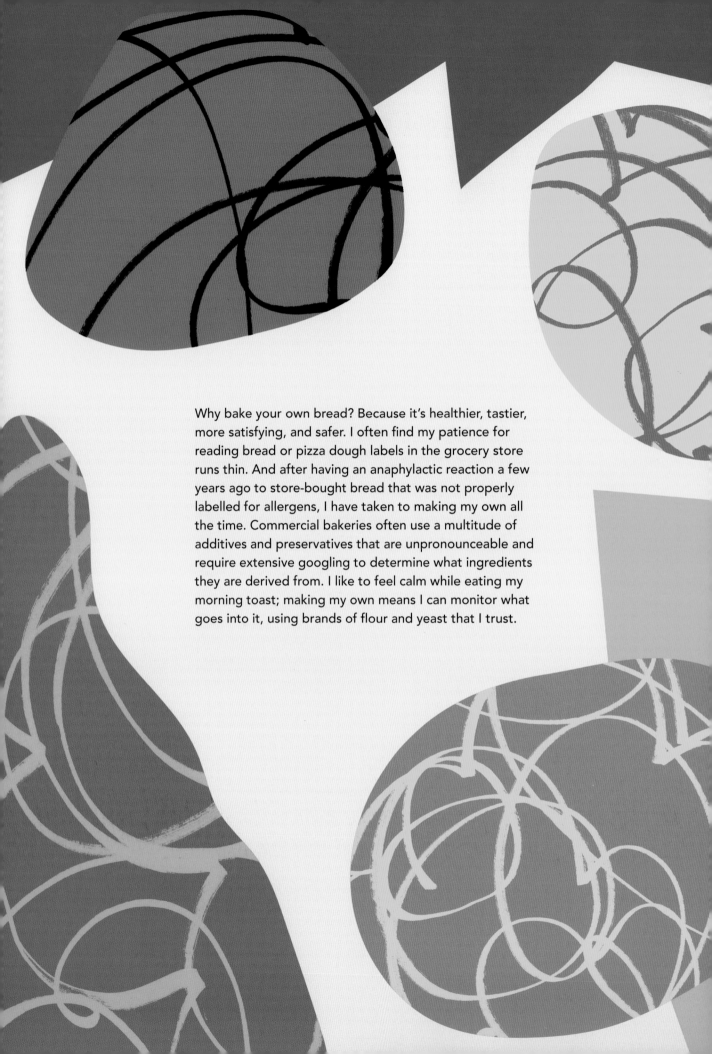

Why bake your own bread? Because it's healthier, tastier, more satisfying, and safer. I often find my patience for reading bread or pizza dough labels in the grocery store runs thin. And after having an anaphylactic reaction a few years ago to store-bought bread that was not properly labelled for allergens, I have taken to making my own all the time. Commercial bakeries often use a multitude of additives and preservatives that are unpronounceable and require extensive googling to determine what ingredients they are derived from. I like to feel calm while eating my morning toast; making my own means I can monitor what goes into it, using brands of flour and yeast that I trust.

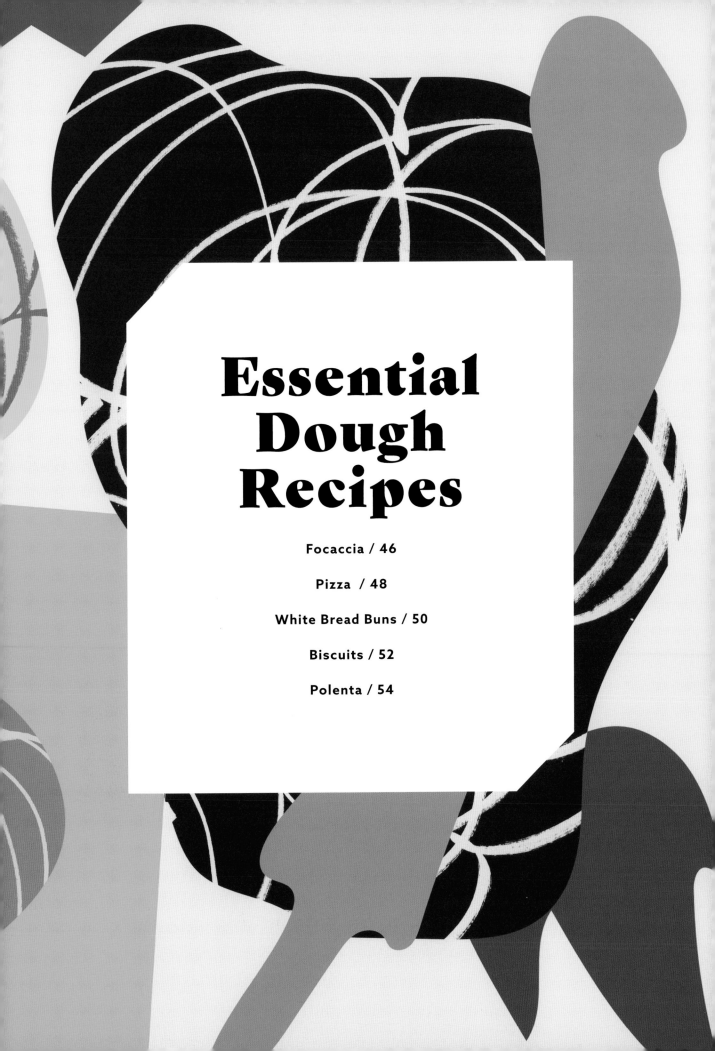

Essential Dough Recipes

Focaccia

Vegetarian (vegan if maple syrup or sugar is used instead of honey)

1½ tsp traditional dry yeast

1¼ cups warm water

2½ cups unbleached all-purpose flour

1½ tsp sea salt

4½ tbsp olive oil (approx), divided

1 tbsp honey

1 clove garlic, finely chopped

1 sprig fresh rosemary or 1 tsp dried rosemary, finely chopped

Dissolve the yeast into the warm water in a small bowl. Let it sit until the yeast becomes puffy and bloated, about 10 minutes.

Meanwhile, mix the flour and salt in a large metal mixing bowl. Make a well in the centre.

Grease another large metal mixing bowl with about 1 tbsp olive oil. Set aside for later; this is where the dough will rise.

When the yeast is ready, pour it into the flour well. Add the honey and 2 tbsp olive oil into the well. Mix the wet ingredients, then begin mixing in the flour around the edges. Work it in until it forms a dough. Knead the dough until it forms a sticky ball. This takes about 1 minute. If the dough begins to feel tough, stop kneading it right away!

Transfer the ball of dough to the oiled bowl and cover it tightly with plastic wrap. Let it rise until it has doubled in size. This takes roughly 1½ hours. Lightly grease an 8-inch non-stick square cake pan (with olive oil) and preheat the oven to 425°F.

When the dough has risen, punch it in the centre. It will deflate right away. Turn it out into the pan and press it out so that it's evenly distributed. Then use your fingertips to press indentations all over the top of the dough. This makes nice little crevices for the olive oil and spices to sit. Let it rise again for 30 minutes, covered with a tea towel.

Drizzle the dough with olive oil, then sprinkle with the finely chopped garlic and rosemary, and sea salt and pepper to taste. Bake at 425°F for 12 minutes, then reduce the heat to 410°F and bake for another 15–18 minutes until golden brown

MAKES 1 (8 X 8-INCH) LOAF

Pizza

Vegetarian (vegan if maple syrup or sugar is used instead of honey)

1 tsp traditional dry yeast

1 cup warm water

2 cups unbleached all-purpose flour

½ cup whole wheat flour

1½ tsp sea salt

2½ tbsp olive oil (approx)

1 tbsp honey

Dissolve the yeast into the warm water in a small bowl. Let it sit until the yeast becomes puffy and bloated, about 10 minutes.

Meanwhile, mix the flours and salt in a large metal mixing bowl. Make a well in the centre.

Grease another large metal mixing bowl with about 1 tbsp olive oil. Set aside for later; this is where the dough will rise.

When the yeast is ready, pour it into the flour well. Add the honey and 1½ tbsp olive oil into the well. Mix the wet ingredients, then begin mixing in the flour around the edges. Work it in until it forms a dough. Knead the dough until it forms a sticky ball. This takes about 1 minute. If the dough begins to feel tough, stop kneading it right away.

Transfer the ball of dough to the oiled bowl and cover it tightly with plastic wrap. Let it rise until it has doubled in size. This takes roughly 1½ hours.

Line 2 baking sheets with parchment paper and preheat the oven to 450°F.

When the dough has risen, punch it in the centre. It will deflate right away. Turn it out onto a large sheet of parchment dusted with flour. Cut it into 4 equal portions. Let it rise again for 30 minutes, covered with a tea towel.

Stretch the dough out into 8-inch rounds, transfer to parchment-lined baking sheets, and add your favourite toppings, like tomato sauce, basil, prosciutto, mushrooms, or sliced peppers. Remember to transfer the dough to the baking sheet before adding toppings or you won't be able to move it! Bake for 10 minutes or until dark brown around the edges.

MAKES 4 PERSONAL PIZZAS

White Bread Buns

Vegetarian (vegan if maple syrup or sugar is used instead of honey)

2¼ tsp traditional dry yeast

2 cups warm water

5 cups unbleached all-purpose flour

1 tbsp sea salt

3 tbsp olive oil (approx)

1 tbsp honey

Dissolve the yeast into the warm water in a small bowl. Let it sit until the yeast becomes puffy and bloated, about 10 minutes.

Meanwhile, mix the flour and salt in a large metal mixing bowl. Make a well in the centre.

Grease another large metal mixing bowl with about 1 tbsp olive oil. Set aside for later; this is where the dough will rise.

When the yeast is ready, pour it into the flour well. Add the honey and 2 tbsp olive oil into the well. Mix the wet ingredients, then begin mixing in the flour around the edges. Work it in until it forms a dough. Knead the dough until it forms a sticky ball. This takes about 1 minute. If the dough begins to feel tough, stop kneading it right away.

Transfer the ball of dough to the oiled bowl and cover it tightly with plastic wrap. Let it rise until it has doubled in size. This takes roughly 1½ hours. Line a baking sheet with parchment paper and preheat the oven to 425°F.

When the dough has risen, punch it in the centre. It will deflate right away. Turn it out onto a large sheet of parchment paper dusted with flour. Use a pastry cutter to cut it into 8 equal portions. Roll each portion into a ball and pinch the bottom so it looks like a bun. Spread these out on the lined baking sheet. It's okay if the edges of the buns touch.

Let them rise again for 30 minutes, covered with a tea towel. Then bake at 425°F for 15 minutes, reduce the heat to 410°F, and bake for another 12–15 minutes. Test if they are done by tapping on the tops; they should sound hollow inside.

Variation
For whole wheat bread, replace 1 cup white flour with 1 cup whole wheat flour.

MAKES 8 BUNS

Tip
Never throw away stale bread! It makes excellent toasts for dipping and snacking, as well as croutons and bread crumbs.

50

Biscuits

Vegetarian if olive oil is used instead of lard

2 cups all-purpose flour

3 tbsp baking powder

1 tsp baking soda

1 tsp salt

⅓ cup lard or olive oil

⅔ cup water

1 tbsp honey mixed with
1 tsp water for glazing

Preheat the oven to 410°F.

Mix the flour, baking powder, baking soda, and salt in a large bowl. Cut the lard into the flour so it forms small pea-sized lumps. If using olive oil, drizzle it around and allow it to clump up with the flour. Make a well in the centre and add the water. Fold the water in gently until it comes together into a ball. Knead the dough 10 times, and then roll it out on a floured surface to ¾-inch thickness. Cut circles out using a water glass or cookie cutter. Brush the tops with the honey solution and place the biscuits on a baking sheet lined with parchment paper. Bake for 8–10 minutes until golden brown.

MAKES 6-8 LARGE BISCUITS

Polenta

3 cups broth or stock

1 cup instant polenta

1 tbsp olive oil

1 tsp salt

Add the broth, cornmeal, olive oil, and salt to a medium-sized pot and turn to low heat. Whisk constantly for 8–10 minutes until it comes together and has a nice smooth consistency. Add more salt to taste. For soft polenta, scoop out and serve hot with your favourite tomato sauce.

For firm polenta, line an 8-inch square cake pan with parchment paper and pour the polenta in. Smooth it out on top, put in the fridge, and chill for 2 hours. Cut the chilled polenta into either fries or cubes and pat dry with paper towel. Heat 2 tbsp of olive oil in a non-stick frying pan. Fry the polenta until it's nice and crispy. Season with salt and serve right away. This makes a great appetizer; you can also use it in place of bread, as the base for a pizza, or serve with pulled pork.

MAKES 9 PERSONAL-SIZED ROUNDS OR 18 THICK FRIES

There are so many options for non-sugar sweeteners and non-dairy milks these days, and with the growing popularity of veganism, there are plenty of new protein sources too. Traditional breakfast favourites like eggs, bacon, and coffee are favourites for a reason. They hit all the major food groups you crave at an indulgent breakfast—caffeine, salty fat, and protein. But there are plenty of other ingredients and foods you can rely on to produce an equally tasty and satisfying meal. Just because you can't have milk doesn't mean you can't have a fancy coffee. An egg allergy doesn't mean you need to miss out on the food porn. And if you don't eat pork or meat in general, you can get that crunch and grease elsewhere.

The "Breakfast" chapter is disproportionately large in this book because I find breakfast and brunch are the meals where people often feel most stumped. A simple fruit salad is always good in my books, but I want to present you some options to mix it up in this chapter. From simple salads, smoothies, and coffees to baked goods and fried treats, your brunches are about to become much more inspired.

Breakfast

Coconut Latte / 58

Cocoa Cinnamon Coffee / 60

Berry Smoothie / 62

Ginger Smoothie / 64

Cucumber, Melon, and Mint Smoothie / 66

Last-Minute Oatmeal / 68

Granola / 70

Chocolate Coconut Spread (on Toast) / 72

Blueberry Scones / 74

Cinnamon Buns / 76

Banana Bread / 78

Make-Ahead Oatmeal Bars / 80

Candied Bacon / 82

Pancakes / 84

Fruit Salad in a Pineapple Boat / 86

Hash Browns / 88

Coconut Latte

Vegetarian (vegan if maple syrup or sugar is used instead of honey)

⅔ cup unsweetened
coconut or rice milk

1 oz shot of espresso

1 tbsp organic honey

Dash of pure vanilla extract

Ground cinnamon for garnish

Add all the ingredients to a small saucepan and simmer on medium heat until steaming. Avoid bringing to a full boil as the milk alternative may separate. Serve hot with a sprinkle of cinnamon. Top with a dollop of Coconut Whipped Cream (page 40) for a rich treat.

While most brands of coconut and rice milk are free from soy, some are not, so please be sure to read the ingredients.

SERVES 1

Cocoa Cinnamon Coffee

Vegetarian and vegan

1 tbsp ground coffee

½ tsp ground cinnamon

½ tsp cocoa powder

2 cups water

Add a little extra flavour to your morning brew with aromatic spices. I love to make this in the winter; it smells cozy and warm.

Add the coffee, cinnamon, and cocoa powder to your coffee maker and brew as you normally would. This recipe works best with a pour-over or a percolator and is fine in a French press if the coffee is not finely ground.

MAKES 2 CUPS

Berry Smoothie

Vegetarian (vegan if maple syrup or sugar is used instead of honey)

Handful of frozen
raspberries (about ½ cup)

¼ cup fresh strawberries,
quartered

¼ cup cold water

Juice of ½ lime (about ½ tbsp)

1 tsp organic honey

Small dash of pure
vanilla extract

Blend all ingredients until smooth and enjoy nice and cold.

SERVES 1

Ginger Smoothie

Vegetarian and vegan

1 banana

½ cup fresh pineapple, roughly diced

¼ cup cold water

Juice of 1 nice, big orange (about ¼ cup)

Juice of ½ lemon (about 1 tbsp)

1 tsp freshly grated ginger

Handful of ice cubes

Blend all ingredients until smooth and enjoy nice and cold.

SERVES 1

Cucumber, Melon, and Mint Smoothie

Vegetarian and vegan

½ cup diced honeydew melon

½ cup cold water

¼ cup diced cucumber
(leave the peel on)

Juice of ½ lime (about ½ tbsp)

2 leaves fresh mint

Handful of ice cubes

Blend all ingredients until smooth and enjoy nice and cold.

SERVES 1

Last-Minute Oatmeal

Vegetarian (vegan if maple syrup or sugar is used instead of honey; for gluten- and wheat-free, use quinoa oats)

½ cup certified gluten-free instant or quick oats

¼ cup boiling water

1 tbsp maple syrup or organic honey (optional)

Flavour combos:

¼ cup each of blueberries, raspberries, and chopped strawberries

1 apple, diced, and ¼ tsp each of cinnamon and ground ginger

1 banana, sliced, 2 tbsp Enjoy Life or other allergen-free chocolate chips, and 1 tbsp sunflower or pumpkin seed butter

Add the oats and any fruits to a cereal bowl and top up with the boiling water. Shake it around to make sure all the oats are moist. Put a plate upside down on top of the bowl so the steam can't escape and let sit for 5 minutes. Remove the plate and fluff with a fork. Add other flavourings such as maple syrup, honey, spices, etc. and mix well.

SERVES 1

Granola

Vegetarian and vegan

1 cup certified gluten-free oats

¼ cup shredded
coconut flakes

¼ cup pumpkin seeds

¼ cup dried cranberries
or raisins

1 tbsp hemp seeds

¼ tsp cinnamon

¼ tsp ground ginger

Light sprinkle of ground cloves

Pinch of salt

Preheat the oven to 375°F and line a baking sheet with parchment paper.

Toss all the ingredients together in a large mixing bowl until they are well combined. Spread the mixture out on the baking sheet and bake for 10 minutes. The spices will become aromatic and the granola will be golden brown.

Serve with your favourite breakfast foods or as a snack on its own.

MAKES ABOUT 1¾ CUPS

Chocolate Coconut Spread (on Toast)

Vegetarian (vegan if maple syrup is used instead of honey)

2 tbsp cocoa powder

1 tbsp coconut oil

½ tbsp honey

Mix all the ingredients together in a small bowl right before you're ready to eat. Mix well and spread on toast or pancakes (page 84). Work quickly because the coconut oil will begin to melt.

MAKES 2 SERVINGS

Blueberry Scones

Vegetarian and vegan if olive oil is used instead of lard

2 cups unbleached
all-purpose flour

3 tbsp baking powder

2 tbsp powdered sugar

½ tsp salt

¼ cup lard or olive oil

1 cup fresh blueberries

¾ cup cold water

Maple syrup

Preheat the oven to 410°F and line a baking sheet with parchment paper.

Add all the dry ingredients to a large bowl and mix until everything is well combined.

If using lard, cut it into the dry ingredients until it forms little pea-sized bits. If using olive oil, drizzle it around the dry ingredients and let it sit for a moment so that it beads together. Mix in the blueberries.

Add the water and mix until it starts to come together into a dough. Then switch to using your hands and knead it 12 times.

Transfer the dough to the lined baking sheet and form into a 6-inch disc. Cut it into 6–8 wedges. Brush with maple syrup as a glaze. Bake for 12 minutes, remove from the oven and pull the wedges apart, then cook for another 5–7 minutes or until golden brown.

Serve warm with jam or alongside a bowl of soup, or tear into them on their own.

MAKES 6-8 SCONES

Cinnamon Buns

Vegetarian (vegan if maple syrup or sugar is used instead of honey)

2 cups warm water

2 tsp traditional dry yeast

3½ cups unbleached all-purpose flour

1 cup whole wheat flour

1 tsp salt

2 tbsp honey

2 tbsp canola oil

Filling:

2 tbsp coconut or canola oil

1 cup dark brown sugar

1 tbsp ground cinnamon

Frosting:

1 cup powdered sugar

2 tbsp water

Extra cinnamon for sprinkling

Add the water and dry yeast to a small bowl and let it sit for about 10 minutes or until the yeast looks puffy.

Add the flours and salt to a large metal mixing bowl and mix well. Make a well in the centre and pour in the puffy yeast and water. Add the honey and oil, and mix all the liquids. Mix with the dry ingredients until it forms a sticky dough. Transfer to a large, greased mixing bowl and cover with plastic wrap. Let it rise until just over double in size, about 1½ hours.

Punch the dough once it has risen and then turn it out onto a surface lined with parchment paper and dusted with flour.

Preheat the oven to 425°F. Roll the dough out into a 24 × 8-inch rectangle. For the filling, brush the whole surface of the dough with the coconut or canola oil and then sprinkle the brown sugar and cinnamon evenly over the top.

Roll it into a log and cut into 12–15 evenly sized rounds. Tuck them snugly into a 9-inch round pie dish, either lined with parchment paper or greased with canola or coconut oil. Bake for 20 minutes, then reduce the heat to 400°F and bake for another 10 minutes.

For the frosting, add the frosting ingredients to a small bowl and mix well. Drizzle the frosting over the warm cinnamon buns before serving.

MAKES 12-15 BUNS

Banana Bread

Vegetarian and vegan

3 very ripe bananas, mashed

1 cup dark brown sugar

⅓ cup applesauce (page 36)

¼ cup canola oil

1½ cups flour

2 tsp baking powder

1½ tsp baking soda

Pinch of salt

Preheat the oven to 350°F and line a 9 x 5-inch loaf pan with parchment paper.

Whisk together the mashed bananas, sugar, applesauce, and oil until smooth. Add the flour, baking powder, baking soda, and salt and fold into the wet ingredients until everything is well combined. Do not overmix. Pour the batter into the loaf pan and bake for 30 minutes or until a toothpick inserted in the centre comes out clean.

MAKES 1 (9 X 5-INCH) LOAF

Make-Ahead Oatmeal Bars

Vegetarian and vegan

1 ripe banana

⅓ cup unsweetened applesauce (page 36)

1½ cups certified gluten-free oats

½ cup shredded coconut flakes (unsweetened)

¼ cup maple syrup

Pinch of salt

1 cup frozen blueberries

Preheat the oven to 375°F and line an 8-inch square cake pan with parchment paper.

Mash the banana and applesauce in a large mixing bowl. Add the oats, coconut, maple syrup, and salt and mix well. Fold in the blueberries. Press the batter into the lined pan and bake for 10–12 minutes until lightly golden. When it's ready, it will appear firm and should not jiggle when you shake the pan. Allow to chill fully before cutting into bars or squares.

MAKES ABOUT 8 BARS

Candied Bacon

1 lb (450g) bacon

¼ cup maple syrup (approx)

Freshly ground black pepper

Preheat the oven to 400°F. Line a rimmed baking sheet with aluminum foil and a sheet of parchment paper. Lay out the bacon evenly on the baking sheet. It's okay if the slices touch or slightly overlap. Drizzle with maple syrup and sprinkle ground black pepper over everything. I like lots of pepper on mine, but the pepperiness is up to you.

Bake for 20 minutes until the bacon is crispy and caramelized. Pat off the excess fat with a paper towel before serving. Enjoy with your favourite breakfast foods.

SERVES 4

Pancakes

1 cup flour

1 tbsp powdered sugar

1 tbsp baking powder

1 tsp baking soda

Pinch of salt

½ cup water

⅓ cup unsweetened applesauce (page 36)

2 tbsp canola oil

Maple syrup and fresh blueberries for serving

Whisk together the flour, sugar, baking powder, baking soda, and salt. Add the water and applesauce and whisk until slightly clumpy and bubbles have begun to form. The batter should appear a little frothy. You can add blueberries or raspberries if you like.

Add the oil to a non-stick frying pan on medium-high heat. Let the oil heat up before spooning in the batter. Check if it's hot enough by dropping in a little bit of batter. It should sizzle when ready. I like to make my pancakes about 3 inches in diameter. Let them cook until bubbles form and pop, leaving indents in the batter, then it's time to flip. They need about 2 minutes on each side and will appear crispy and golden brown when done.

Serve hot with maple syrup and fresh blueberries.

SERVES 2

Fruit Salad in a Pineapple Boat

Vegetarian (vegan if maple or agave syrup is used instead of honey)

1 ripe pineapple

1 cup mixed berries

½ cup diced papaya

½ cup diced apple or pear

Juice of 1 lime (about 1 tbsp)

5 leaves mint, torn

Drizzle of honey

Cut the pineapple in half and carve the centre out of each half, leaving the stem intact. Dice the flesh into cubes and toss with the rest of the fruit in a large bowl, along with the lime juice, mint leaves, and honey. Spoon it back into the pineapple for a fresh-looking presentation. Feel free to use whatever fruit is in season where you live; it always tastes best.

Hash Browns

Vegetarian and vegan

2 russet potatoes

2 tbsp olive or canola oil

Salt and pepper to taste

Shred the potatoes (no need to peel them) and pile them all up in a paper towel. Squeeze the paper towel to get rid of the excess water and pat the shreds dry. Heat the oil in a non-stick frying pan and when it's nice and hot, add the potato in an even layer. Season with salt and pepper to taste. When the edges look crispy and the potato has turned soft and translucent, flip it over (in one piece if you can!) and fry the other side for several minutes until nice and crisp. Transfer to a plate and serve hot, with a side salad of arugula and sliced avocado tossed in a little olive oil and lemon juice.

SERVES 2

This chapter is all about my favourite thing: veggies! From salads to roasted vegetables, sandwiches, and lunch ideas, this chapter covers 13 tasty ways to get your daily servings of nutritional goodness. I have at least one salad every day, and I usually try to bring both a hot and a cold veggie dish to work for lunch. Heartier veggies such as sweet potatoes and kale pack a real punch of energy to keep you going all day. And my alternative to grilled cheese is so fresh and delicious, I could eat it any time, any day.

This chapter has many options for vegetarians and vegans, and easy substitutes to make recipes suitable for such diets. There's at least one person (but generally several) with a diet free of meat or animal products in each of my social circles, so it's important to me to know how to make dishes for them that are filling and flavourful.

I'm allergic to all legumes and soy, which includes peanuts, most beans, peas, chickpeas, lentils, soybeans (edamame), miso, tamari, and tofu. I also avoid leaves of legumes such as fenugreek, rooibos, bean sprouts, and pea shoots. This undoubtedly makes vegetarian or vegan dining a challenge for me, but when cooking at home there are ways around it. Seeds and quinoa are excellent sources of protein. I often sprinkle hemp or pumpkin seeds on my veggie meals just before serving. Cooked quinoa can be added as a garnish or used in place of rice for the base of a dish.

Veggies & Greens

ROASTING

Most allergic people spend a disproportionate amount of time in the kitchen, since takeout and restaurant options can be very limited. Roasting is the best way to cook for yourself on nights when you really wish you didn't have to. It's the simplest and surest way to make a flavourful, nutritious meal that usually doubles as leftovers for lunch the next day.

To make cleaning easier, line the pan with aluminum foil before laying down a sheet of parchment paper, if the recipe you're making is a bit oily. In general, you can anticipate that any hearty vegetable, including potatoes, sweet potatoes, yams, and cauliflower, will take about 45 minutes to brown and cook through in a 375°F oven. Ensure everything is evenly coated in olive or canola oil and season with salt and pepper to taste. (See the recipe for Caramelized Roasted Veggie Medley on page 100.)

Green veggies, such as broccoli, zucchini, or asparagus, and peppers will take less time and tenderize quickly, in about 25 minutes. (See the recipe for Lemony Asparagus on page 104.) Broccoli florets should be cut into ½-inch pieces for quick cooking time.

Roasted Veggie Sandwich

Vegetarian (vegan if maple syrup or sugar is used instead of honey in the bread recipe)

1 zucchini, sliced lengthwise

1 red bell pepper, cut into quarters, or 1 portion Italian-Style Roasted Peppers (page 102)

1 portobello mushroom, sliced

Olive oil

Salt and pepper to taste

4 slices focaccia (page 46) or white bread buns (page 50)

1 tbsp grainy or Dijon mustard

8 leaves fresh basil

1 tbsp chopped fresh parsley

Toss all the veggies in a light coating of olive oil and season with salt and pepper to taste. Spread them out on a baking sheet lined with parchment paper and roast at 400°F for 25–30 minutes or until they are crispy and browned.

Broil or toast the bread if you prefer. Spread the mustard, and add the fresh herbs evenly. Layer on the roasted veggies and the top piece of bread or focaccia.

MAKES 2 SANDWICHES

Open-Faced Summer Veggie Sandwich

Vegetarian (vegan if maple syrup or sugar is used instead of honey in the bread recipe)

2 thick slices of white
bread buns (page 50)

½ avocado

3–4 slices heirloom
or cherry tomatoes

3 leaves fresh basil

1 green onion, chopped

1 tsp olive oil

Coarse salt and pepper
to taste

Toast the bread. Mash up the avocado and spread it on the bread. Arrange the tomatoes and basil on the bread, sprinkle on the green onions, drizzle the olive oil over top, and season with salt and pepper to taste.

SERVES 1

Grilled Avocado Sandwich

Vegetarian (vegan if maple syrup or sugar is used instead of honey in the bread recipe)

1 avocado

1 tsp Dijon mustard

1 tsp + 1 tbsp olive oil

1 tsp lemon or lime juice

3–4 leaves fresh basil

Salt and pepper to taste

2 slices of white bread buns (page 50)

Blend the avocado, mustard, 1 tsp olive oil, citrus juice, basil, salt and pepper in a blender or food processor until smooth. Spread it on 1 slice of bread and pop the other slice on top. Press down firmly without squishing the bread.

Heat 1 tbsp olive oil in a non-stick frying pan. Fry the sandwich until crispy, then flip over and fry until crispy on the other side. It takes about 3 minutes per side. Slice the sandwich in half and serve hot.

SERVES 1

Caramelized Roasted Veggie Medley

Vegetarian and vegan

2 sweet potatoes

2 large yellow or red potatoes

2 large carrots

1 red onion

1½ cups brussels sprouts

1 zucchini

1 red bell pepper

2 cups cherry tomatoes

5 cloves garlic, peeled

2 sprigs fresh rosemary

1 tbsp olive oil

Sea salt and freshly ground black pepper to taste

Wedge of lemon or Meyer lemon for serving

Preheat the oven to 375°F.

Peel and chop the sweet potatoes, potatoes, carrots, and red onion into 1-inch cubes. Peel and halve the sprouts, cut the zucchini into half-moons, and cut the pepper into 1-inch chunks. The tomatoes and garlic should stay whole. The rosemary can be snipped into smaller sections. Toss everything in a light coating of olive oil and spread it out evenly on a baking sheet lined with parchment paper. Season with salt and pepper.

Roast for 25 minutes, then remove the garlic cloves and mash them up. Toss all the veggies and the mashed garlic, spread out evenly on the baking sheet, and return to the oven for another 25 minutes or until everything is caramelized and crispy around the edges.

Serve with a wedge of lemon or Meyer lemon.

SERVES 2-4

100

Italian-Style Roasted Peppers

Vegetarian and vegan

4 bell peppers (preferably red, orange, or yellow as they are the sweetest)

1 tsp olive oil, plus a little more if you are roasting peppers in the oven

¼ cup julienned basil leaves

1 clove garlic, finely chopped

1 tsp balsamic vinegar

Salt and pepper to taste

On the grill: If you have a charcoal or gas grill, roast the peppers, whole, on the grill on high heat with the lid closed until the skins turns completely black. Flip them over every couple of minutes so that all sides get cooked evenly. Once the peppers are blackened, put them in a metal bowl and cover immediately with aluminum foil to allow them to steam for a few minutes. This will help the skins slip off more easily. When they're cool enough to touch, peel the skins off and remove the stems and seeds. Cut the pepper flesh into thin strips and toss with the oil, basil, garlic, vinegar, and salt and pepper to taste.

In the oven: Preheat oven to 375°F. Cut the peppers in half and remove the seeds and stems. Toss lightly in olive oil and spread out evenly on a baking sheet lined with parchment paper. Sprinkle salt and pepper on top. Roast for 40 minutes or until the edges are caramelized and golden. Slice the peppers into strips, leaving the skin intact, and toss with the basil, garlic, and vinegar, and add more salt and pepper to taste.

Serve hot or cold, with polenta (vegan, page 54) or white bun toast (vegan if made without honey; contains wheat, page 50).

MAKES 6-8 STARTER/APPETIZER PORTIONS

Tip
The peppers can be roasted ahead of time and kept in the fridge until ready to serve.

Lemony Asparagus

Vegetarian and vegan

1 bunch asparagus, trimmed

1 tbsp olive oil

Sea salt and pepper to taste

Juice of 1 lemon
(about 2 tbsp)

1 tbsp balsamic vinegar

Zest of ½ lemon (about 1 tsp)

¼ cup chopped basil

Preheat the oven to 400°F and line a baking sheet with parchment paper.

Spread the asparagus out on the baking sheet and drizzle with olive oil, salt and pepper. Squeeze the lemon juice over the spears. Roast for 25–30 minutes.

Drizzle the balsamic over the roasted spears and then sprinkle on the lemon zest and basil. Serve warm.

SERVES 2-4

Spiced Roasted Carrots

Vegetarian (vegan if maple syrup is used instead of honey)

6–8 carrots, stems on

1 tbsp olive oil

½ tsp salt

½ tsp ground black pepper

½ tsp turmeric

¼ tsp cinnamon

Optional:

¼ cup pomegranate seeds

2 green onions, chopped

1 tbsp honey

Preheat the oven to 375°F and line a baking sheet with parchment paper.

Wrap the stems of the carrots with aluminum foil to prevent them from burning. Mix the olive oil, salt, pepper, turmeric, and cinnamon in a small bowl. Brush or drizzle it over the carrots and spread them out on the baking sheet. Roast for 45 minutes or until golden brown.

I like to dress them up with pomegranate seeds, chopped green onions, and a bit of honey. You can leave the carrots whole or cut them into chunks and toss it all together as a salad.

SERVES 2

Pomegranate Salad
with Saffron Dressing

Vegetarian (vegan if maple or agave syrup is used instead of honey)

1 head Boston lettuce

½ cup pomegranate seeds

¼ cup blueberries

1 orange, peeled and cut into segments

5 leaves fresh basil

4 sprigs dill, torn

2 tbsp olive oil

Juice of ½ lemon (about 1 tbsp)

1 tsp honey

¼ tsp saffron strands

Salt to taste

Tear the lettuce into large chunks and toss with the pomegranate seeds, blueberries, orange, basil, and dill. Mix the olive oil, lemon juice, honey, saffron, and salt in a small bowl. The dressing should turn a rich orange colour. Drizzle it over the salad and mix well.

SERVES 2

Weeknight Salad

½ head iceberg lettuce, chopped

2 radishes, sliced

1 avocado, sliced

⅓ cup sliced cucumbers

¼ cup canned corn

3 or 4 slices of prosciutto (read the ingredients and use the packaged kind, not sliced at the deli counter)

¼ cup olive oil or avocado oil

1 tbsp lemon juice or white wine vinegar

¼ tsp salt

The ingredients and measurements in this recipe do not need to be exact. Feel free to use peppers or mushrooms if you have them in your fridge; romaine or Boston lettuce is an easy substitute for iceberg, if you're craving a more flavourful green. Toss all the ingredients together and enjoy right away.

SERVES 6

Apple and Kale Slaw

Vegetarian (vegan if maple or agave syrup is used instead of honey)

Dressing:

1 avocado

⅓ cup olive oil

3 tbsp apple cider vinegar

1 tbsp Dijon mustard*

1 tbsp honey

1 tsp salt

½ tsp black pepper

3 cups shredded
Savoy cabbage

2 cups shredded Tuscan kale,
stems removed

1 Granny Smith apple,
cut into sticks

1 carrot, shaved
and sliced into sticks

Blend all the dressing ingredients together until creamy and smooth. Toss with the cabbage, kale, apple, and carrot so everything is well coated. For the best taste and texture, let it sit in the fridge for at least 1 hour before serving.

SERVES 2

*Dijon mustard can sometimes contain gluten.

Tangy Beets

Vegetarian (vegan if maple or agave syrup is used instead of honey)

6 medium-sized beets

1 tbsp olive oil

1 tbsp aged balsamic vinegar

1 tsp apple cider vinegar

1 tsp honey

Salt and freshly ground black pepper to taste

Handful of arugula for serving

Pumpkin or hemp seeds for garnish (optional)

Wrap the whole beets (minus the stems) in foil and roast on a baking sheet at 375°F for 1 hour. Let them come to room temperature and then peel and cut into quarters.

Toss with the olive oil, vinegars, and honey. Add salt and pepper to taste. Pour it all over a bed of arugula and add pumpkin or hemp seeds, if you wish.

SERVES 2

Fennel and Arugula Salad

Vegetarian and vegan

Dressing:

¼ cup olive oil

Juice of 1 lemon
(about 2 tbsp)

1 tbsp apple cider vinegar

½ tsp sea salt

¼ tsp black pepper

1 head fennel, cut
into thin rounds

4½ cups baby arugula

Mix all the dressing ingredients in a small bowl. Pour it over the fennel and arugula and toss well. I like to start out with half the dressing and add more if needed.

SERVES 4

Berry and Avocado Summer Salad

Vegetarian and vegan

1 avocado, diced

¼ cup quartered strawberries

¼ cup blueberries

¼ cup raspberries

3–4 leaves mint, ripped

3 leaves fresh basil, ripped

1 tbsp olive oil

½ tbsp balsamic vinegar

¼ tsp each of salt and freshly ground black pepper

Add all the ingredients to a bowl and mix well.

While avocado and berries are neither greens nor veggies, this savoury salad recipe pairs well with proteins. This is one of my favourite things to eat for lunch!

SERVES 1

I'm a big fan of slow roasting a piece of meat and then using every part of it for meals throughout the week. Nothing goes to waste in my home. Chicken carcasses always become broth; leftover meat is sliced or pulled for sandwiches or soup. If I'm making bacon for breakfast, I'll often make a few extra pieces and use them for lunch on a sandwich, with leftover chicken breast from dinner the night before. It's both economical and practical to waste as little as possible—both food and your own time. This way, there's always something ready to assemble in the fridge.

Protein

Chicken Sandwich / 122

Sweet Chicken Wings / 124

Chicken Lettuce Wraps / 126

Stovetop Pulled Pork / 128

Grilled Blade Steak with Chopped Tomatoes,
Herbs, and Green Onions / 130

Crispy Baked Salmon / 132

Roasted Fillet of Sole / 134

Tuna and Radish Salad / 136

Slow-Roasted Lamb with Cranberry Sauce / 138

One-Pan Roast Chicken Dinner / 140

Roast Beef with Mushroom Gravy / 142

Chicken Sandwich

2 slices of white
bread buns (page 50)

Olive oil for drizzling

Salt to taste

1 avocado

1 cooked chicken breast

2 strips cooked smoky bacon

Sauce:

1 tbsp Dijon mustard

1 tbsp honey or maple syrup

Drizzle slices of bread with olive oil and salt to taste, and toast in the oven on the broil setting until crispy.

Cut the avocado into slices or mash with a fork, whatever you prefer. Cut the chicken breast into thin slices. Use the leftover breast from my One-Pan Roast Chicken Dinner (page 140) or roast a chicken breast brushed with olive oil, thyme, and salt at 375°F for 25 minutes.

For the sauce, mix the Dijon and honey or maple syrup together in a small bowl.

To assemble, spread the sauce on both pieces of toast, fan the avocado out if sliced or spread it if mashed, lay several slices of chicken on top, and then pile on the bacon and final layer of bread.

MAKES 1 SANDWICH

Sweet Chicken Wings

½ cup orange juice

¼ cup organic honey

1 tbsp freshly chopped garlic

1 tbsp peeled, chopped fresh ginger

1 tsp salt

½ tsp black pepper

3 pounds chicken wings, split

¼ cup chopped mint

¼ cup chopped cilantro

Chili flakes (optional)

Preheat the oven to 375°F and line a baking sheet with aluminum foil and a layer of parchment paper for easy cleanup.

Blend the juice, honey, garlic, ginger, salt, and pepper, and toss with the wings so they are evenly coated. Spread the wings out on the baking sheet and bake for 30 minutes. Flip the wings and bake for another 30 minutes, then flip again and broil for 3 minutes or until crispy. Toss with the herbs and add chili flakes if desired.

SERVES 2-4

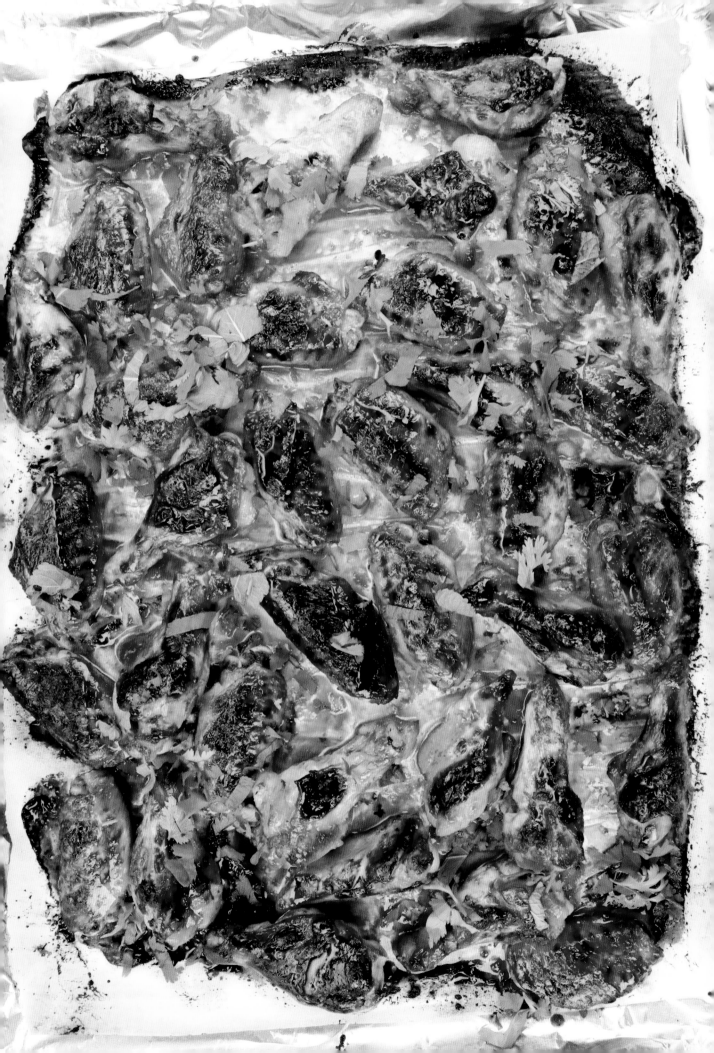

Chicken Lettuce Wraps

1 roasted chicken breast

1 bell pepper, diced

¼ cup diced heirloom
cherry tomatoes

2 green onions, finely sliced

1 tbsp sun-dried tomatoes,
finely chopped (optional)

2 tsp olive or avocado oil

1 tsp balsamic vinegar

Salt and pepper to taste

4 large leaves
of Boston lettuce

Reserve 1 chicken breast from the One-Pan Roast Chicken Dinner (page 140), or roast a chicken breast brushed with olive oil, black pepper, and salt at 375°F for 25 minutes. Slice thinly when cooled.

Toss the chicken with the red pepper, cherry tomatoes, green onions, sun-dried tomatoes (if using), oil, and balsamic, and season with salt and pepper to taste. Layer 2 leaves of lettuce together and fill with the chicken salad.

MAKES 2 WRAPS

Stovetop Pulled Pork

1 pork shoulder (about ⅓ lb)

2 large carrots,
cut into big chunks

1 large onion,
cut into big chunks

3 cloves garlic

3 sprigs thyme

4 leaves sage

1 tbsp salt

Sauce:

3 tbsp dark brown sugar

3 tbsp pure tomato paste

1½ tbsp apple cider vinegar

1 tbsp paprika

1 tbsp balsamic vinegar

½ tsp cayenne pepper

Add the pork, carrots, onion, garlic, thyme, sage, and salt to a large pot and cover with water. Simmer with the lid askew for 6 hours. Pull the pork out of the pot and shred it using two forks. Remove any bones or large pieces of fat that would be unpleasant to bite into. Transfer the pulled pork to another pot, add all the sauce ingredients, and stir well. Simmer for 20 minutes to allow all the flavours to sink in. Serve with Apple and Kale Slaw (page 112).

SERVES 4

128

Grilled Blade Steak with Chopped Tomatoes, Herbs, and Green Onions

2 cups roughly chopped cherry or cocktail tomatoes

10 large leaves fresh basil, julienned (approx)

5 green onions, finely chopped

2 tbsp chopped dill

1 tbsp balsamic vinegar

1 tbsp avocado or olive oil + additional olive oil for brushing

Salt to taste

1 lb blade steak

1 garlic clove

The salad
Toss the tomatoes, basil, green onions, dill, vinegar, oil, and salt. Set aside to marinate while you prepare the meat.

The steak
Use a charcoal grill for the best flavour! Rub the steak all over with a garlic clove cut in half. Brush with oil and salt to taste, and sear on a hot grill for a few minutes on each side. If you don't have a grill, you can use a frying pan, but beware: It can be messy. Let the meat rest for 5 minutes before slicing into strips. Serve warm over top of the tomato salad.

SERVES 2

Crispy Baked Salmon

1 4-5 oz salmon fillet

¼ tsp salt

1 tsp ground black pepper

Olive or canola oil for the pan

1 tbsp maple syrup

1 tbsp organic honey

Wedge of lemon
or lime for serving

Preheat the oven to 375°F and line a baking dish with parchment paper. Season both sides of the salmon with the salt and pepper.

Heat some olive or canola oil in a non-stick frying pan. When it's hot, place the salmon in and let it sear for 3 minutes on high heat until crispy. Flip and sear the other side. Transfer to the lined baking dish. Mix the maple syrup and honey in a small bowl and brush it all over the fillet. Bake for 9–12 minutes. It should be crisp on the outside and slightly pink on the inside.

Serve with roasted or steamed asparagus and avocado.

SERVES 1

Roasted Fillet of Sole

1 fillet of sole (about 4 oz)

1 tsp olive or avocado oil

Leaves of 2–3 sprigs
fresh thyme

Salt and pepper to taste

Several slices of lemon

Preheat the oven to 375°F.

Lay out a sheet of parchment paper and place the fish in the centre. Brush the oil on both sides, and sprinkle with the fresh thyme leaves, salt, and pepper to taste. Place the lemon slices on top, then take the sides of the parchment paper and roll them up together to create an oblong package. Transfer it to a baking sheet and bake for about 20 minutes until fish is opaque white with lightly browned edges.

Serve with a light, fresh salad.

SERVES 1

Tuna and Radish Salad

1 can (5 oz) tuna packed
in olive oil

2 radishes, thinly sliced

1 sprig fresh dill,
finely chopped

1 green onion, finely chopped

1 tsp apple cider vinegar

Freshly ground black pepper

Boston or romaine lettuce
leaves for serving

Mix the first six ingredients together and serve in a lettuce cup. This packs really well for a quick breakfast or lunch.

SERVES 1

Slow-Roasted Lamb with Cranberry Sauce

2 carrots, cut into large chunks

1 lb mini yellow potatoes

½ red onion, cut into quarters

5 garlic cloves, peeled

3–4 sprigs fresh rosemary

1 leg of lamb (bone-in, about 5 lb)

1 tbsp olive oil

½ tsp each of sea salt and black pepper

2 tbsp grainy Dijon mustard*

¼ cup balsamic vinegar

Cranberry sauce:

2 cups fresh or frozen cranberries

¼ cup orange juice

3 tbsp dark brown sugar

¼ tsp cinnamon

Pinch of salt

Preheat the oven to 350°F.

Line a roasting pan with the carrots, potatoes, onion, garlic, and rosemary. Place the lamb on top and pat it dry. Brush with the olive oil and season with the salt and black pepper. Brush a thick coat of mustard on the lamb. Pour balsamic into the roasting tray so it covers the vegetables in the bottom.

Cover the whole thing in aluminum foil and bake for 4–5 hours. Then remove the foil and broil until the meat is crispy, about 2–3 minutes. Pull the meat apart and serve with a scoop of the vegetables.

For the cranberry sauce, add all the ingredients to a pot and bring to a boil, then turn down to low and simmer for about 20–30 minutes. Stir often to prevent sticking and to mash the cranberries down. Serve hot with the lamb.

SERVES 4 WITH LEFTOVERS

*Dijon mustard can sometimes contain gluten.

One-Pan Roast Chicken Dinner

4 large carrots, cut into ½-inch chunks

1½ lb baby yellow potatoes, or yellow potatoes cut into quarters

1½ cups cherry tomatoes

½ onion, cut into chunks

5 cloves garlic, unpeeled

5 sprigs fresh thyme

1 whole chicken (about 2 lb)

3 tbsp olive oil

1 tsp salt

1 tsp black pepper

Gravy:

¼ cup white wine*

Juice of 1 lemon (about 2 tbsp)

2 tbsp organic honey

1 tbsp Dijon mustard** (optional)

Preheat the oven to 400°F. Spread the carrots, potatoes, cherry tomatoes, onion, garlic, and thyme out in the bottom of a roasting pan, preferably cast iron. Pat the chicken skin dry and lay the chicken on top of the vegetables. Brush the skin with olive oil, making sure to coat all the nooks and crannies. Sprinkle salt and pepper all over the bird, on all sides. Roast for 20 minutes, then turn the bird on its side, toss the veggies around in the fat and juices, and return to the oven for another 20 minutes. Repeat this until all four sides have been roasted and the bird is golden brown all over. For an extra-crispy exterior, brush the breasts with maple syrup or organic honey and roast for an additional 5–10 minutes.

Allow the bird to rest for 30 minutes before cutting it into sections.

For the gravy, drain the pan juices into a small saucepan and add the wine, lemon juice, honey, and mustard (if using). Smash the roasted garlic cloves to remove the peels and add to the pot as well. Simmer on medium heat, whisking often, until reduced and fragrant. This should take about 15 minutes.

Serve chicken with roasted vegetables and gravy.

SERVES 4

* Ensure the wine does not contain casein, egg, or fish products by checking with the company. Allergen labelling is not required on alcoholic drinks.
** Dijon mustard can sometimes contain gluten.

Roast Beef with Mushroom Gravy

2 lb strip loin roast

2 tbsp olive oil, divided

2 cloves garlic, peeled

3–4 sprigs fresh rosemary

3–4 leaves fresh sage

1 tbsp balsamic vinegar

1 can or bottle of beer*
(preferably a lager)

1½ cups sliced mushrooms

1 tsp salt

Freshly ground black pepper

Preheat the oven to 350°F.

Sear the beef in a non-stick frying pan in about 1 tbsp of the olive oil. Brown it on all sides. Transfer to a large roasting pan and add the whole garlic cloves, rosemary, sage, balsamic vinegar, and beer (use homemade vegetable or chicken stock instead of beer for a wheat-free version), and salt. Cover with foil and bake for 4 hours, then remove the cover, brush some of the fat overtop, and broil until the top is crispy, about 2 minutes.

Remove the roast and let it rest for at least 25 minutes before slicing.

Sauté the mushrooms (I use a mix of button, oyster, and shiitake) in the remaining 1 tbsp olive oil in a non-stick frying pan until they're browned and soft. Pour in the pan juices from the beef and turn to medium-high heat; add salt and pepper to taste. Simmer until reduced by a third. Skim any extra oil off the top and then transfer to a gravy boat. Slice the beef thinly and serve with the hot mushroom gravy, roasted potatoes, and a salad for a simple and easy entertaining idea.

SERVES 4

*Ensure the beer does not contain allergens by checking with the company. Allergen labelling is not required on alcoholic drinks.

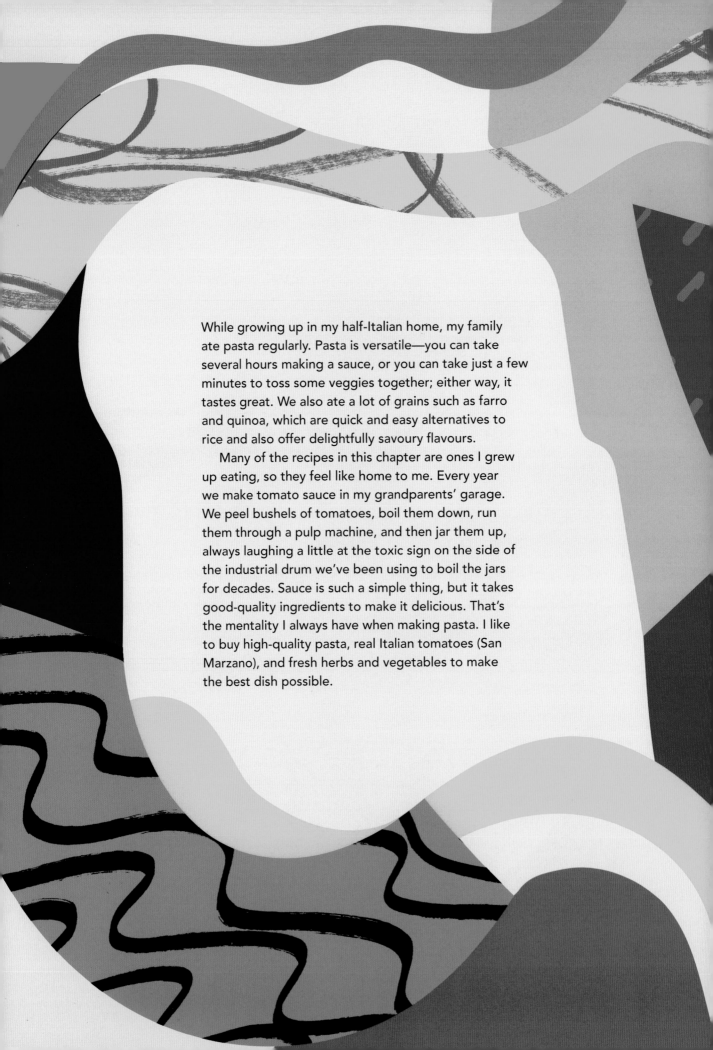

While growing up in my half-Italian home, my family ate pasta regularly. Pasta is versatile—you can take several hours making a sauce, or you can take just a few minutes to toss some veggies together; either way, it tastes great. We also ate a lot of grains such as farro and quinoa, which are quick and easy alternatives to rice and also offer delightfully savoury flavours.

Many of the recipes in this chapter are ones I grew up eating, so they feel like home to me. Every year we make tomato sauce in my grandparents' garage. We peel bushels of tomatoes, boil them down, run them through a pulp machine, and then jar them up, always laughing a little at the toxic sign on the side of the industrial drum we've been using to boil the jars for decades. Sauce is such a simple thing, but it takes good-quality ingredients to make it delicious. That's the mentality I always have when making pasta. I like to buy high-quality pasta, real Italian tomatoes (San Marzano), and fresh herbs and vegetables to make the best dish possible.

Pasta & Grains

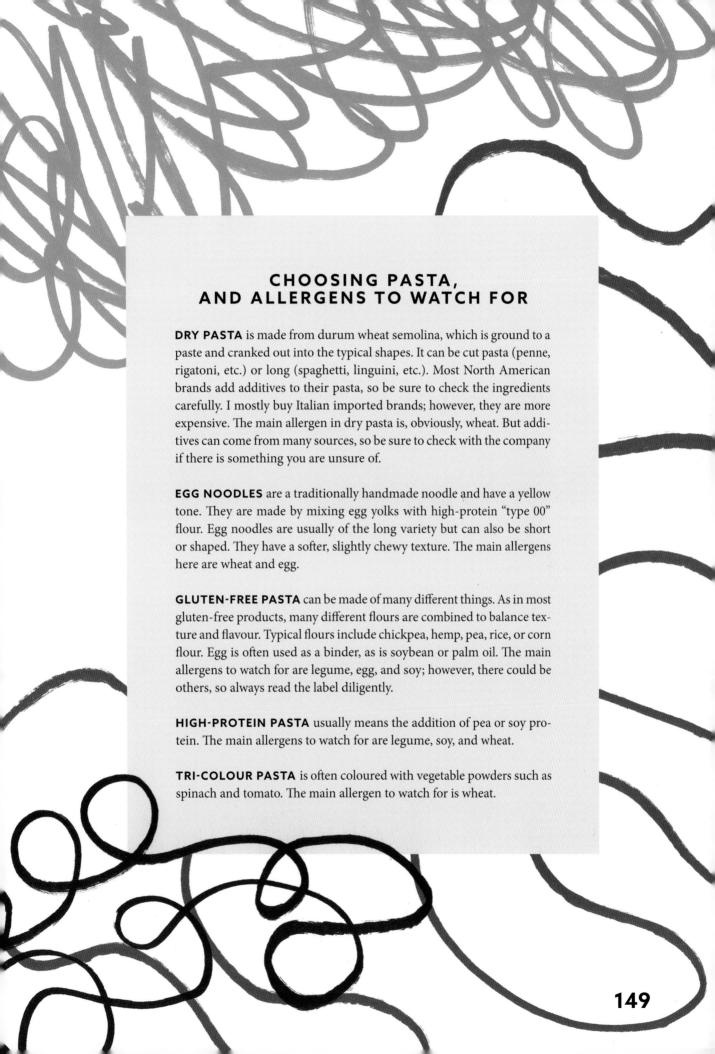

CHOOSING PASTA,
AND ALLERGENS TO WATCH FOR

DRY PASTA is made from durum wheat semolina, which is ground to a paste and cranked out into the typical shapes. It can be cut pasta (penne, rigatoni, etc.) or long (spaghetti, linguini, etc.). Most North American brands add additives to their pasta, so be sure to check the ingredients carefully. I mostly buy Italian imported brands; however, they are more expensive. The main allergen in dry pasta is, obviously, wheat. But additives can come from many sources, so be sure to check with the company if there is something you are unsure of.

EGG NOODLES are a traditionally handmade noodle and have a yellow tone. They are made by mixing egg yolks with high-protein "type 00" flour. Egg noodles are usually of the long variety but can also be short or shaped. They have a softer, slightly chewy texture. The main allergens here are wheat and egg.

GLUTEN-FREE PASTA can be made of many different things. As in most gluten-free products, many different flours are combined to balance texture and flavour. Typical flours include chickpea, hemp, pea, rice, or corn flour. Egg is often used as a binder, as is soybean or palm oil. The main allergens to watch for are legume, egg, and soy; however, there could be others, so always read the label diligently.

HIGH-PROTEIN PASTA usually means the addition of pea or soy protein. The main allergens to watch for are legume, soy, and wheat.

TRI-COLOUR PASTA is often coloured with vegetable powders such as spinach and tomato. The main allergen to watch for is wheat.

Spaghettini with Tomatoes

Vegetarian and vegan

2 tbsp olive oil

1 clove peeled garlic, finely chopped

3 sun-dried tomatoes, cut into strips

Fresh chilies, finely chopped, to taste

5–6 leaves fresh basil, plus additional basil for garnish

2 cups cherry tomatoes or hothouse tomatoes, chopped

Salt and pepper to taste

2 cups cooked spaghettini

Heat the olive oil in a non-stick frying pan and add the garlic. Fry until fragrant, then add the sun-dried tomatoes, fresh chilies (if you prefer it to be spicy), and the basil. Let simmer for 1 minute, then add the tomatoes, salt, and pepper. Let simmer on medium heat for about 10 minutes, until the tomatoes are softened and reduced. Add the cooked spaghettini and toss well. Sprinkle some fresh basil on top before serving.

SERVES 2

Fusilli with Mushrooms and Asparagus

Vegetarian and vegan

2 tbsp olive oil

1 clove garlic, finely chopped

2 cups chopped mushrooms

½ cup chopped asparagus

2 cups cooked fusilli

½ cup chopped basil

½ cup chopped parsley

4–5 leaves mint, roughly chopped

2 tbsp chopped chives

Juice of 1 lemon (about 2 tbsp)

Heat the olive oil in a non-stick frying pan and add the finely chopped garlic. Fry until it becomes fragrant, then add the mushrooms and asparagus. Fry on medium-high heat until golden brown and softened. Add the cooked fusilli, basil, parsley, mint, chives, and lemon juice and toss well. Let it simmer on low in the pan for a few minutes, then serve hot.

SERVES 2

The Best Tomato Sauce

Vegetarian and vegan

2 cloves peeled garlic

1 tbsp olive oil

1 can (27 oz) San Marzano tomatoes

2 leaves fresh basil

Salt to taste

Fry the garlic in the olive oil until it becomes fragrant, then add the tomatoes and basil immediately. Always use whole plum tomatoes. Bring to a boil and then turn down to medium low, put the lid on askew, and wait 2 hours. Season with salt to taste periodically. Mash the tomatoes with a fork partway through, and be sure to stir occasionally. Can be used in everything from pastas to stews and soups.

MAKES 2½ CUPS

Penne with Pesto

Vegetarian and vegan

2 bell peppers

⅓ cup, +
1 tsp olive oil, divided

2 cups fresh basil leaves

1 cup julienned Tuscan kale,
stems and thick veins removed

1 clove garlic, peeled

½ tsp salt + more to taste

¼ tsp black pepper

4 cups cooked penne rigate

Cut the bell peppers into strips and stir-fry until crispy in a non-stick frying pan with 1 tsp olive oil.

Blend the basil, kale, garlic, ⅓ cup olive oil, ½ tsp salt, and pepper in a blender until smooth.

Toss the cooked penne, peppers, and pesto so that everything is evenly coated and combined. Add salt to taste.

SERVES 4

Linguini with Tomatoes and Cauliflower

Vegetarian and vegan

2 tbsp olive oil

½ head of cauliflower, broken into small florets

Salt to taste

2 cups whole plum tomatoes, preferably San Marzano

Pinch of saffron

2 cups cooked linguini

Chopped fresh parsley, basil, or microgreens

Heat the olive oil in a large non-stick frying pan and add the cauliflower. Season well with salt. Fry on high until crispy, then turn down to low and add the tomatoes and saffron. Let simmer for 30–45 minutes. Toss with the cooked pasta and chopped parsley, basil or microgreens for colour.

SERVES 2

Lemon and Dill Wheat Bulgur

Vegetarian and vegan

2 cups water

1 cup wheat bulgur

½ cup olive oil

Juice of 1 lemon
(about 2 tbsp)

Zest of ½ lemon (about 1 tsp)

1 tbsp chopped dill

1 tbsp Dijon mustard*

1 tsp salt

½ tsp black pepper

Bring the water and wheat bulgur to a boil and then reduce and let summer with lid on for 15 minutes. While it's cooking, add all the remaining ingredients to a small bowl and mix well. Fluff the bulgur with a fork after cooking and add as much of the dressing as you prefer.

SERVES 4

*Dijon mustard can sometimes contain gluten.

Maple Quinoa

Vegetarian and vegan

2 cups cooked quinoa
(your choice of white,
red, black, or mixed)

1 apple, diced

½ cup celery, chopped

¼ cup pumpkin seeds
(optional)

2 tbsp maple syrup

1 tbsp olive oil

1 tsp apple cider vinegar

¼ tsp ground ginger

Salt and black pepper to taste

Toss the cooked quinoa with the apple, celery, and pumpkin seeds (if using). In a small bowl, mix the maple syrup, oil, cider vinegar, ginger, salt, and pepper. Pour the dressing over the quinoa mixture and toss well.

Prepare ahead of time and chill in the fridge until ready to eat. This makes a perfect lunch for work.

MAKES 4 LUNCH-SIZED SERVINGS

Green Rice Bowl

Vegetarian and vegan

2 cups cooked brown
or wild rice

1 avocado, pitted,
peeled, and sliced

1 green apple, diced

1 pear, diced

⅓ cup diced cucumber

Juice of 1 lime (about 1 tbsp)

1 tbsp olive oil

1 tsp finely chopped
fresh ginger

½ tsp salt

Handful of cilantro

A few mint leaves, chopped

Line the base of a soup bowl with the rice. Add the avocado, apple, pear, and cucumber in sections on top.

Mix the lime juice, olive oil, ginger, and salt in a small bowl and drizzle it over everything. Sprinkle the cilantro and mint over top.

SERVES 2

Farro with Prosciutto, Carrot, and Zucchini

1 tbsp olive oil

1 clove garlic, finely chopped

½ cup diced carrot

¼ cup roughly chopped prosciutto

1 cup diced zucchini

1 cup halved cherry tomatoes

3–4 leaves fresh basil, ripped

Salt and pepper to taste

2 cups cooked farro

Heat the olive oil over medium heat in a large frying pan and add the chopped garlic. Sauté until fragrant, then add the carrot and prosciutto and cook until softened and browned. Add the zucchini, cherry tomatoes, and basil and fry on medium heat until everything is cooked through and is a nice golden-brown colour. The cherry tomatoes should be soft and saucy. Add the cooked farro and mix well. Let it simmer over medium-low heat for a few minutes to absorb all the flavours of the sauce.

SERVES 2

Heirloom Cherry Tomatoes and Bitter Greens Orecchiette

Vegetarian and vegan

5 cups orecchiette or other cut pasta (penne or short rigatoni also works well)

1½ cups roughly chopped heirloom cherry tomatoes

2½ cups baby spinach

2½ cups baby arugula

¼ cup olive oil

2 tbsp balsamic vinegar

Salt and pepper to taste

This recipe is ready in the time it takes to cook the pasta! And it makes a perfect lunch.

Boil the pasta according to package directions. Add the tomatoes to a bowl with the greens. Pour the hot, drained pasta over the tomatoes and greens so that they wilt slightly. Add the olive oil, balsamic, salt, and pepper and toss.

SERVES 4-6

I've always been really into baking. I take pleasure in recipes with lots of steps that take all day to prepare. But I also appreciate a quick, simple recipe that doesn't take much practice to perfect. Nearly every baked good or dessert I consume is one that I've made myself, and I enjoy baking for others as often as possible. Desserts are meant to be moments of bliss, and that's what I aim to create with each recipe in this chapter.

It's a common misconception that sweets are improved with more butter, more eggs, more nuts, and so on. But really there are so many other ingredients that make a dessert flavourful and rich, or light and delicate. I use a lot of fruit and veggies in my baking, and it often surprises my taste testers!

Desserts

Chocolate Bark

Vegetarian and vegan

1 cup allergen-free chocolate chips, such as Enjoy Life

½ tsp pure vanilla extract

¼ tsp cinnamon

¼ tsp ground ginger

¼ cup salted, shelled pumpkin seeds

¼ cup shredded coconut flakes

Pinch of sea salt

Melt the chocolate and vanilla in a double boiler or in the microwave. Mix well to ensure the vanilla is evenly distributed. Mix in the cinnamon and ginger. Line a baking sheet with parchment paper. Pour the chocolate onto the parchment and spread it out into a ¼-inch-thick sheet. Sprinkle the pumpkin seeds, coconut flakes, and salt evenly over the top. Refrigerate for at least 1 hour and then smash it up into pieces by dropping it on the counter. Keep in the fridge until ready to serve.

MAKES 4 SERVINGS

Variation
Replace the pumpkin seeds and coconut flakes with ¼ cup dried cranberries and 1 tsp orange zest.

Banana Brownie Cookies

Vegetarian and vegan

2 ripe bananas

½ cup powdered sugar

2 tbsp brown sugar

½ tsp pure vanilla extract

Pinch of salt

1¼ cups allergen-free chocolate chips, such as Enjoy Life

1 cup whole wheat or unbleached all-purpose flour

1 tsp baking soda

Preheat the oven to 375°F and line a baking sheet with parchment paper. Mash the bananas with the powdered sugar, brown sugar, vanilla, and salt. Set aside.

Melt the chocolate either in the microwave or in a double boiler. As soon as it's fully melted, whisk in the banana mixture until smooth. Add the flour and baking soda, and use a spatula to mix the batter until it is just combined.

Dampen your fingers and pull off chunks of the batter, which should be a bit firm. Roll each piece into a ball and space them 2 inches apart on the baking sheet. Press the tops down gently with the palm of your hand.

Bake for 8–10 minutes until the cookies have risen and settled.

MAKES 12 COOKIES

Blueberry Lemon Squares

Vegetarian if shortening is used instead of lard

Filling:

3½ cups frozen blueberries (1 bag)

½ cup powdered sugar

2 tbsp maple syrup

Juice of 1 lemon (about 2 tbsp)

½ tsp lemon zest

Crust:

1 cup whole wheat flour

1 cup unbleached all-purpose flour

¾ cup powdered sugar

½ tsp salt

⅔ cup lard or shortening

2 tbsp coconut oil

¼ cup unsweetened applesauce (page 36)

1 tbsp maple syrup

Preheat the oven to 375°F and line an 8-inch square cake pan with parchment paper.

For the filling, simmer the blueberries, powdered sugar, 2 tbsp maple syrup, lemon juice, and zest on medium-low heat for 40 minutes, stirring often.

For the crust, combine the flours, sugar, and salt in a large mixing bowl. Cut the lard or shortening and the coconut oil into the flour so that it forms little pea-sized bits throughout. Add the applesauce and 1 tbsp maple syrup and mix until it comes together into a rough dough.

Press the dough into the lined cake pan, and then spoon the blueberry filling on top in an even layer. Bake for 20 minutes until the berry mixture has bubbled and then settled. Let it cool fully before cutting into squares.

MAKES 9 SQUARES

Roasted Fruit with Thyme

Vegetarian (vegan if maple syrup is used instead of honey)

3–4 peaches, cut in halves

1 cup strawberries, stems removed

½ cup raspberries

½ cup blueberries

3 tbsp organic honey

½ tsp cinnamon

½ tsp pure vanilla extract

Leaves of 1–2 sprigs fresh thyme

Pinch of salt

Preheat the oven to 375°F and line a baking sheet with parchment paper.

Spread the peaches and berries out on the baking sheet. In a small bowl, mix the honey, cinnamon, vanilla, thyme, and salt. Drizzle the honey mixture evenly over the fruit. Bake for 30 minutes until the fruit is caramelized, oozing juices, and very fragrant. Serve hot. Pairs well with your favourite allergy-friendly ice cream.

SERVES 4

Chocolate Pots

Vegetarian (vegan if maple syrup is used instead of honey)

1 large sweet potato

2 tbsp coconut milk

1 tbsp organic honey

1 tsp coconut oil

½ tsp pure vanilla extract

Pinch of salt

1½ cups allergen-free chocolate, such as Enjoy Life

Garnish:

pomegranate seeds, mint leaves, or berries

Wash the sweet potato and poke a hole in the skin with a knife. Wrap it up in parchment paper or aluminum foil and roast at 375°F for 1½ hours, until syrupy and silky in texture. Unwrap and let it come to room temperature. Roast the sweet potato ahead of time for best results.

Blend ¾ cup of the roasted sweet potato flesh with the coconut milk, honey, coconut oil, vanilla, and salt, until smooth and creamy.

Melt the chocolate either in a double boiler or in the microwave. Fold the chocolate into the sweet potato batter so that no streaks of orange remain. Spoon it out into individual servings and chill in the fridge for at least 1 hour before serving. Garnish with pomegranate seeds and mint leaves, or your favourite berries.

MAKES 4 SERVINGS

Variations
Use banana instead of sweet potato for a more pudding-like consistency.
Use avocado instead of sweet potato for a denser, thicker texture.

Mixed Berry Pie

Vegetarian if coconut oil is used instead of lard
(vegan if maple syrup is used instead of honey)

Filling:

2 cups strawberries, stems removed, flesh roughly chopped

2 cups blueberries

2 cups raspberries

2 cups blackberries

¼ cup maple syrup or honey

2 tbsp powdered sugar

2 tbsp water

½ tsp pure vanilla extract

Crust:

2 cups flour

¼ cup powdered sugar

½ tsp salt

¾ cup lard or coconut oil

½ cup cold water

Garnishes:

Fresh berries

Coconut Whipped Cream (page 40)

For the filling, add all filling ingredients to a pot and simmer on medium low for 1 hour, or until thick and syrupy. Stir often to prevent it from sticking or burning.

For the crust, add the flour, sugar, and salt to a large mixing bowl and mix well. Cut in the lard or coconut oil so it forms small pea-sized balls. Make a well in the centre and add the cold water. Mix the dry ingredients in and form into a ball. Knead 6 times and shape into a disc. Wrap in parchment and refrigerate for 1 hour.

Preheat the oven to 375°F.

Roll the dough out to a ¼-inch-thick round and press into a 9-inch pie pan. This recipe makes a bottom crust only, but there is enough to do a design on top if desired. Pinch the edges using your fingers or a fork. Pour the filling in and brush with maple syrup diluted with some water to make it brushable. Bake for 35–40 minutes until the top is browned and crispy.

Let it cool completely, for several hours at least, before slicing. Top it with fresh berries and serve with Coconut Whipped Cream (page 40).

Seed Butter Cups

Vegetarian (vegan if maple syrup is used instead of honey)

½ cup allergen-free chocolate, such as Enjoy Life

¼ cup sunflower seed butter, such as SunButter (or substitute Pumpkin Seed Butter, page 38)

1 tbsp honey or maple syrup

Line a mini muffin tin with foil muffin cups.

Melt the chocolate in a double boiler or in the microwave. Pour a spoonful into each muffin cup so it's filled about halfway.

Mix the sunflower seed butter and honey or maple syrup in a small bowl, then add a small dollop to each of the cups. Pour more chocolate into each cup to fill to the top. Chill for at least 1 hour before serving to allow them to harden.

MAKES ABOUT 10 SMALL CUPS

P N D E W S F SF C

"Nutty" Chocolate Spread

Vegetarian (vegan if maple or agave syrup is used instead of honey)

2 tbsp cocoa powder

1 tbsp sunflower seed butter

½ tbsp coconut oil

½ tbsp honey

Mix all the ingredients together in a small bowl right before you're ready to eat. Mix well and spread on toast or pancakes (page 84). Work quickly because the coconut oil will begin to melt.

MAKES 2 SERVINGS

Blueberry Vanilla Layer Cake

Vegetarian and vegan if coconut oil is used instead of lard

²⁄₃ cup unsweetened applesauce (page 36)

¼ cup canola oil

1 cup powdered sugar

¼ cup lemon juice

¼ cup coconut milk

Pinch of salt

2 cups flour

2 tsp baking powder

1½ tsp baking soda

Frosting:

½ cup lard or coconut oil

¼ cup lemon juice

1 tsp pure vanilla extract

5–6 cups powdered sugar

¼ cup coconut milk

Decoration:

fresh blueberries

lemon zest

Preheat the oven to 375°F and line two 6-inch round cake pans with parchment paper.

In a large mixing bowl, whisk together the applesauce, oil, 1 cup powdered sugar, lemon juice, coconut milk, and salt. Add the flour, baking powder, and baking soda and beat well, making sure to scrape the sides of the bowl down.

Pour the cake batter evenly into the two pans and bake for 20 minutes or until a toothpick inserted in the centre comes out clean. Let the cooked cakes cool on a rack. They should be completely cooled before you begin frosting. I even leave them in the fridge overnight.

For the frosting, add the lard or coconut oil, lemon juice, and vanilla to a large mixing bowl. Beat well. Add 5–6 cups powdered sugar, ½ cup at a time, alternating with the coconut milk, 1 tbsp at a time. Continue beating until it is frothy and light.

To assemble, shave the round tops off the cakes using a long knife. Try to make this as even as possible or you'll end up with a crooked cake. Add a layer of frosting on top of the first layer, then stick a few toothpicks in the centre and place the top layer on. The toothpicks will keep the top layer from sliding off or shifting. Cover the top of the cake in a thin layer of frosting called the "crumb layer" and let it set in the fridge. When it has firmed up, frost the top of the cake with a liberal amount of frosting. Pile some fresh blueberries on the centre and grate lemon zest on top for colour.

Cocoa Zucchini Loaf

Vegetarian and vegan if coconut oil is used instead of lard

3 cups all-purpose flour

⅓ cup pure cocoa powder

4 tsp baking powder

3 tsp baking soda

Pinch of salt

1 cup dark brown sugar

⅓ cup lard, coconut oil, or vegetable oil

2 tbsp molasses

1 tsp pure vanilla extract

2 cups grated zucchini

1 cup unsweetened applesauce (page 36)

½ cup water

1 cup allergen-free chocolate chips, such as Enjoy Life (optional)

Preheat the oven to 350°F and line two 8½ x 5-inch loaf pans with parchment paper.

Whisk the dry ingredients (flour through salt) together and set aside.

Cream the sugar, lard or oil, molasses, and vanilla in a large mixing bowl. Add the zucchini, applesauce, and water, and whisk well. Sift in the dry ingredients to break up any lumps, then mix until just combined. Be careful not to overmix. Fold in the chocolate chips (if using).

Divide the batter equally into the loaf pans. Bake for 35–40 minutes, or until a toothpick inserted in the centre comes out clean.

MAKES 2 (8½ × 5 INCH) LOAVES

This chapter is full of all the things I usually eat when I need a quick snack or bite of something flavourful, but don't really need a whole meal. Since there are few fast-food or takeout spots that I can rely on, I often just need a bite of something I can quickly throw together at home to satisfy my cravings. These are all just ideas/ inspirations, so the measurements do not have to be exact by any means. Some people may reach for chips or a cookie to snack on, but I like to throw together one of these hasty, tasty snacks.

Not-Even-Recipes / Stuff to Nom On

Nine Ways to Eat an Avocado

Vegetarian (vegan if you omit honey)

Cut the avocado in half and remove the pit. Use a knife to score it, leaving gaps for the flavours to sit in:

- Cinnamon and honey

- Dipped in lots of poppy seeds

- Dipped in shelled hemp seeds, drizzled with olive oil, and sprinkled with coarse salt

- A smear of sunflower or pumpkin seed butter and honey

- Tomato guts and salt

- A sprinkle of cocoa and drizzle of maple syrup

- Paprika, coriander, and fresh cilantro

- Basil and mashed raspberry

- Lime juice and cayenne pepper

Sweet, Salty, Crunchy

Vegetarian (vegan if maple or agave syrup is used instead of honey)

1 apple, cut into slices

2 tbsp sunflower
or pumpkin seed butter

1 tsp honey or maple syrup

Pinch each of salt, cinnamon,
turmeric, and cayenne pepper

Slice the apple into rounds and top with either sunflower or pumpkin seed butter, honey or maple syrup, and the salt, cinnamon, turmeric, and cayenne pepper. Ready in under 2 minutes!

SERVES 1

BBQ-Flavoured Popcorn

Vegetarian and vegan

5 cups popped popcorn

1 tbsp olive oil

1 tsp paprika

½ tsp ground rosemary

½ tsp salt

¼ tsp finely ground
black pepper

Put the popcorn in a large bowl, drizzle with the olive oil, and sprinkle on the paprika, rosemary, salt, and pepper. For a sweet twist, add either a drizzle of honey or maple syrup.

SERVES 2

Blender Sorbet

Vegetarian (vegan if simple syrup, agave syrup, or maple syrup is used instead of honey)

1 banana

1 cup frozen raspberries (or your choice of berry)

2 tbsp honey

2 tbsp cold water

1 tsp vanilla

Add all the ingredients to a blender and pulse until just blended. I like to leave some chunks in mine, but the texture is up to you. It should be thick and dense—perfect to eat with a spoon.

SERVES 1

Spiced Citrus

Vegetarian and vegan

¼ tsp ground ginger

¼ tsp turmeric

Pinch of pink salt or
flaky sea salt

Freshly ground black pepper

1 orange, sliced in half

1 grapefruit, sliced in half

Sprinkle ginger, turmeric, salt, and pepper over the slices of grapefruit and oranges for a quick, tasty snack.

SERVES 1-2

Creamy Hot Chocolate

Vegetarian (vegan if maple or agave syrup is used instead of honey)

1 heaping tbsp pure
cocoa powder

1 heaping tbsp honey

1 cup light coconut milk

¼ cup water

Add the cocoa and honey to a small pot and mix until it becomes creamy. Slowly mix in the coconut milk and water. Turn the heat on medium and stir constantly until heated through, about 5 minutes. Do not let it come to a boil or it will separate. Serve hot.

SERVES 1

204

Acknowledgments

Thank you to my husband, Brandon, my brother, John, and my parents, Theresa and Marcello. Thank you to the Yazdani squad, especially Lili and Jake, for taste testing and always adding extra chocolate! Thank you, Karrie and Jessey, for your encouragement and for modelling for this book. And again to Karrie Kwong for contributing some beautiful photos. Thanks to Amanda Gauthier for coming up with this brilliant title. Thank you to the *Everyday Allergen-Free* team for your hard work. Thanks to my agent, Kelvin Kong (K2 Literary), my publisher, Taryn Boyd, editor Meg Yama-moto, proofreader Paula Marchese, and the team at TouchWood Editions. Thank you, Tree Abraham, for the beautiful design work. Thanks for the support and encouragement of my former colleagues on the Print team at Indigo Books & Music, and to all my friends and family members who have supported me in this project. And a big thank you to all the food allergy bloggers, vloggers, writers, and parents who work to educate others about food allergies.

Suggested Reading

Everyday Allergen-Free Blog Posts to Consider

https://www.everydayallergenfree.com/home/teens-adults-food-allergies-events

https://www.everydayallergenfree.com/home/2017/3/2/food-allergies-the-alternative-facts

https://www.everydayallergenfree.com/home/2017/4/18/its-super-awkward-to-turn-down-a-kiss

https://www.everydayallergenfree.com/home/2017/5/17/yolo-so-carry-your-epi-pen

https://www.everydayallergenfree.com/home/2017/8/29/heading-to-university-or-college-this-week?rq=university

Bloggers to Follow

Allergy Awesomeness: https://allergyawesomeness.com/

Allergy Girl Eats: https://www.allergygirleats.com/

Allergy Travels: https://allergytravels.com/

Allergylicious: https://allergylicious.com/

FARE: https://www.foodallergy.org/

Food Allergy Canada: http://foodallergycanada.ca/

Friendly Pantry: https://www.friendlypantry.com/

My Kid's Food Allergies: https://mykidsfoodallergies.com/

No Nuts Moms Group: https://nonutsmomsgroup.weebly.com/

Nut-Free Wok: http://www.nutfreewok.com/

Nutritionally Nicole: https://www.nutritionallynicole.com/

The Allergy Mom: http://theallergymom.com/

Miss Allergic Reactor: http://www.missallergicreactor.com/

Turn It Teal: https://www.turnitteal.org/blog/

Free from:

	PEANUT	NUT	DAIRY	EGG	SOY	WHEAT	FISH	SHELLFISH	COCONUT	VEGETARIAN	VEGAN
BASIC RECIPES											
Chicken Broth	✓	✓	✓	✓	✓	✓	✓	✓	✓	✗	✗
Vegetable Broth	✓	✓	✓	✓	✓	✓	✓	✓	✓	✓	✓
Salad Dressings	✓	✓	✓	✓	✓	✓	✓	✓	✓	✓	✓
Strawberry Jam	✓	✓	✓	✓	✓	✓	✓	✓	✓	✓	OPTION
Applesauce	✓	✓	✓	✓	✓	✓	✓	✓	✓	✓	✓
Pumpkin Seed Butter	✓	✓	✓	✓	✓	✓	✓	✓	✓	✓	OPTION
Coconut Whipped Cream	✓	✓	✓	✓	✓	✓	✓	✓	✗	✓	OPTION
ESSENTIAL DOUGH RECIPES											
Focaccia	✓	✓	✓	✓	✓	✗	✓	✓	✓	✓	OPTION
Pizza	✓	✓	✓	✓	✓	✗	✓	✓	✓	✓	OPTION
White Bread Buns	✓	✓	✓	✓	✓	✗	✓	✓	✓	✓	OPTION
Biscuits	✓	✓	✓	✓	✓	✗	✓	✓	✓	OPTION	OPTION
Polenta	✓	✓	✓	✓	✓	✓	✓	✓	✓	OPTION	OPTION
BREAKFAST											
Coconut Latte	✓	✓	✓	✓	✓	✓	✓	✓	✗	✓	OPTION
Cocoa Cinnamon Coffee	✓	✓	✓	✓	✓	✓	✓	✓	✓	✓	✓
Berry Smoothie	✓	✓	✓	✓	✓	✓	✓	✓	✓	✓	OPTION
Ginger Smoothie	✓	✓	✓	✓	✓	✓	✓	✓	✓	✓	✓
Cucumber, Melon, and Mint Smoothie	✓	✓	✓	✓	✓	✓	✓	✓	✓	✓	✓
Last-Minute Oatmeal	✓	✓	✓	✓	✓	✓	✓	✓	✓	✓	OPTION
Granola	✓	✓	✓	✓	✓	✓	✓	✓	✗	✓	✓
Coconut Chocolate Spread	✓	✓	✓	✓	✓	✓	✓	✓	✗	✓	OPTION
Blueberry Scones	✓	✓	✓	✓	✓	✗	✓	✓	✓	OPTION	OPTION
Cinnamon Buns	✓	✓	✓	✓	✓	✗	✓	✓	✗	✓	OPTION
Banana Bread	✓	✓	✓	✓	✓	✗	✓	✓	✓	✓	✓
Make-Ahead Oatmeal Bars	✓	✓	✓	✓	✓	✓	✓	✓	✗	✓	✓
Candied Bacon	✓	✓	✓	✓	✓	✓	✓	✓	✓	✗	✗
Pancakes	✓	✓	✓	✓	✓	✗	✓	✓	✓	OPTION	OPTION
Fruit Salad in a Pineapple Boat	✓	✓	✓	✓	✓	✓	✓	✓	✓	✓	OPTION
Hash Browns	✓	✓	✓	✓	✓	✓	✓	✓	✓	✓	✓
VEGGIES & GREENS											
Roasted Veggie Sandwich	✓	✓	✓	✓	✓	✗	✓	✓	✓	✓	OPTION
Open-Faced Summer Veggie Sandwich	✓	✓	✓	✓	✓	✗	✓	✓	✓	✓	OPTION
Grilled Avocado Sandwich	✓	✓	✓	✓	✓	✗	✓	✓	✓	✓	OPTION

Free from:	PEANUT	NUT	DAIRY	EGG	SOY	WHEAT	FISH	SHELLFISH	COCONUT	VEGETARIAN	VEGAN
Caramelized Roasted Veggie Medley	✓	✓	✓	✓	✓	✓	✓	✓	✓	✓	✓
Italian-Style Roasted Peppers	✓	✓	✓	✓	✓	✓	✓	✓	✓	✓	✓
Lemony Asparagus	✓	✓	✓	✓	✓	✓	✓	✓	✓	✓	✓
Spiced Roasted Carrots	✓	✓	✓	✓	✓	✓	✓	✓	✓	✓	OPTION
Pomegranate Salad with Saffron Dressing	✓	✓	✓	✓	✓	✓	✓	✓	✓	✓	OPTION
Weeknight Salad	✓	✓	✓	✓	✓	✓	✓	✓	✓	✗	✗
Apple and Kale Slaw	✓	✓	✓	✓	✓	✓	✓	✓	✓	✓	OPTION
Tangy Beets	✓	✓	✓	✓	✓	✓	✓	✓	✓	✓	OPTION
Fennel and Arugula Salad	✓	✓	✓	✓	✓	✓	✓	✓	✓	✓	✓
Berry and Avocado Summer Salad	✓	✓	✓	✓	✓	✓	✓	✓	✓	✓	✓

PROTEIN

	PEANUT	NUT	DAIRY	EGG	SOY	WHEAT	FISH	SHELLFISH	COCONUT	VEGETARIAN	VEGAN
Chicken Sandwich	✓	✓	✓	✓	✓	✗	✓	✓	✓	✗	✗
Sweet Chicken Wings	✓	✓	✓	✓	✓	✓	✓	✓	✓	✗	✗
Chicken Lettuce Wraps	✓	✓	✓	✓	✓	✓	✓	✓	✓	✗	✗
Stovetop Pulled Pork	✓	✓	✓	✓	✓	✓	✓	✓	✓	✗	✗
Grilled Blade Steak with Chopped Tomatoes, Herbs, and Green Onions	✓	✓	✓	✓	✓	✓	✓	✓	✓	✗	✗
Crispy Baked Salmon	✓	✓	✓	✓	✓	✓	✗	✓	✓	✗	✗
Roasted Fillet of Sole	✓	✓	✓	✓	✓	✓	✗	✓	✓	✗	✗
Tuna and Radish Salad	✓	✓	✓	✓	✓	✓	✗	✓	✓	✗	✗
Slow-Roasted Lamb with Cranberry Sauce	✓	✓	✓	✓	✓	✓	✓	✓	✓	✗	✗
One-Pan Roast Chicken Dinner	✓	✓	✓	✓	✓	✓	✓	✓	✓	✗	✗
Roast Beef with Mushroom Gravy	✓	✓	✓	✓	✓	✗	✓	✓	✓	✗	✗

PASTA & GRAINS

	PEANUT	NUT	DAIRY	EGG	SOY	WHEAT	FISH	SHELLFISH	COCONUT	VEGETARIAN	VEGAN
Spaghettini with Tomatoes	✓	✓	✓	✓	✓	✗	✓	✓	✓	✓	✓
Fusilli with Mushrooms and Asparagus	✓	✓	✓	✓	✓	✗	✓	✓	✓	✓	✓
The Best Tomato Sauce	✓	✓	✓	✓	✓	✓	✓	✓	✓	✓	✓
Penne with Pesto	✓	✓	✓	✓	✓	✗	✓	✓	✓	✓	✓
Linguini with Tomatoes and Cauliflower	✓	✓	✓	✓	✓	✗	✓	✓	✓	✓	✓
Heirloom Cherry Tomatoes and Bitter Greens Orecchiette	✓	✓	✓	✓	✓	✗	✓	✓	✓	✓	✓
Lemon and Dill Wheat Bulgur	✓	✓	✓	✓	✓	✗	✓	✓	✓	✓	✓
Maple Quinoa	✓	✓	✓	✓	✓	✓	✓	✓	✓	✓	✓

	PEANUT	NUT	DAIRY	EGG	SOY	WHEAT	FISH	SHELLFISH	COCONUT	VEGETARIAN	VEGAN
Green Rice Bowl	✓	✓	✓	✓	✓	✓	✓	✓	✓	✓	✓
Farro with Prosciutto, Carrot, and Zucchini	✓	✓	✓	✓	✓	✗	✓	✓	✓	✗	✗

DESSERTS

	PEANUT	NUT	DAIRY	EGG	SOY	WHEAT	FISH	SHELLFISH	COCONUT	VEGETARIAN	VEGAN
Chocolate Bark	✓	✓	✓	✓	✓	✓	✓	✓	✗	✓	✓
Banana Brownie Cookies	✓	✓	✓	✓	✓	✗	✓	✓	✓	✓	✓
Blueberry Lemon Squares	✓	✓	✓	✓	OPTION	✗	✓	✓	✗	OPTION	✗
Roasted Fruit with Thyme	✓	✓	✓	✓	✓	✓	✓	✓	✓	✓	OPTION
Chocolate Pots	✓	✓	✓	✓	✓	✓	✓	✓	✗	✓	OPTION
Mixed Berry Pie	✓	✓	✓	✓	✓	✗	✓	✓	✗	✓	OPTION
Seed Butter Cups	✓	✓	✓	✓	✓	✓	✓	✓	✓	✓	OPTION
"Nutty" Chocolate Spread	✓	✓	✓	✓	✓	✓	✓	✓	✗	✓	OPTION
Blueberry Vanilla Layer Cake	✓	✓	✓	✓	✓	✗	✓	✓	✗	✓	OPTION
Cocoa Zucchini Loaf	✓	✓	✓	✓	✓	✗	✓	✓	✗	✓	OPTION

NOT-EVEN-RECIPES /STUFF TO NOM ON

	PEANUT	NUT	DAIRY	EGG	SOY	WHEAT	FISH	SHELLFISH	COCONUT	VEGETARIAN	VEGAN
Nine Ways to Eat an Avocado	✓	✓	✓	✓	✓	✓	✓	✓	✓	✓	OPTION
Sweet, Salty, Crunchy	✓	✓	✓	✓	✓	✓	✓	✓	✓	✓	OPTION
BBQ-Flavoured Popcorn	✓	✓	✓	✓	✓	✓	✓	✓	✓	✓	✓
Blender Sorbet	✓	✓	✓	✓	✓	✓	✓	✓	✓	✓	OPTION
Spiced Citrus	✓	✓	✓	✓	✓	✓	✓	✓	✓	✓	✓
Creamy Hot Chocolate	✓	✓	✓	✓	✓	✓	✓	✓	✗	✓	OPTION

Index

Amanda Orlando is the creator of EverydayAllergenFree.com, which she started to inspire confidence in people who live with life-threatening food allergies and dietary restrictions. Her writing has appeared in the Huffington Post, and she is the author of *Allergen-Free Desserts to Delight Your Taste Buds* (Skyhorse Publishing, 2015). She lives in Toronto.